lonely

POCKET

AUSTIN

TOP EXPERIENCES • LOCAL LIFE

T0276711

AMY BALFOUR,
REGIS ST LOUIS, GREG WARD

Contents

Plan Your Trip 4

Texas State Capitol (p34)
SKY NOIR PHOTOGRAPHY BY BILL DI/GETTY IMAGES ©

Explore Austin 31

Special Features

Survival Guide 145

COVID-19

We have re-checked every business in this book before publication to ensure that it is still open after the COVID-19 outbreak. However, the economic and social impacts of COVID-19 will continue to be felt long after the outbreak has been contained, and many businesses, services and events referenced in this guide may experience ongoing restrictions. Some businesses may be temporarily closed, have changed their opening hours and services, or require bookings; some unfortunately could have closed perma-nently. We suggest you check with venues before visiting for the latest information.

Austin's Top Experiences

See government in action at Texas State Capitol (p34)

Remember the Alamo at Bob Bullock Texas State History Museum (p36)

Watch the nightly bat swarm under Congress Avenue Bridge (p66)

Become a Longhorn for a day at the University of Texas (p92)

Explore San Antonio's historic icon: the Alamo (p130)

Stroll along San Antonio's River Walk (p132)

Climb the 102 steps of Mt Bonnell (p114)

Discover the flora of Texas at Lady Bird Johnson Wildflower Center (p70)

Look and learn at Lyndon Baines Johnson (LBJ) Library & Museum (p90)

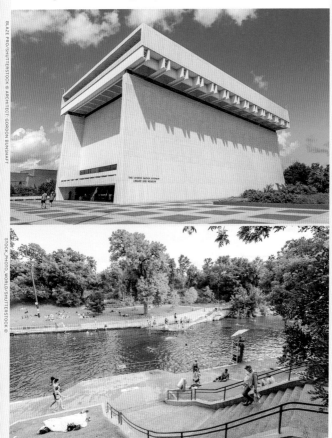

BLAZE PRO/SHUTTERSTOCK © ARCHITECT: GORDON BUNSHAFT

STOCK_PHOTO_WORLD/SHUTTERSTOCK ©

Enjoy the outdoors at Zilker Park (p68)

Dining Out

The Austin food scene is innovative and downright delicious. Barbecue and Tex-Mex are mainstays, but fine-dining restaurants and world cuisines abound. Downtown eateries are a mixed bag, serving tourists, business folks, politicians, artists and night-owl clubbers. South Austin and East Austin have lots of interesting choices, including amazing food trucks. Around the UT campus prices drop – but often so does quality.

Food Trucks

From epicurean Airstreams to regular old taco trucks, food trailers are kind of a big deal in Austin, and wandering from one to another is a fun way to experience the local food scene. Because of their transient nature, we haven't listed any of these rolling restaurants, but since they travel in packs, we can tell you where they tend to congregate.

South Austin Trailer Park and Eatery This seems to be a rather settled trailer community, with a fence, an official name, a sign and picnic tables.

East Austin This area has its own little enclave, conveniently located right among all the bars on the corner of E 6th and Waller Sts.

Rainey Street A cluster of food trucks is ready to serve the downtown hordes downing beers at nearby bars.

Best Cheap Eats

Hopdoddy Burger Bar Join the line for gourmet burgers. (p78)

Veracruz All Natural Food truck that sells tacos so popular they hand you a buzzer. (p58)

Home Slice Stop by before or after South Congress fun for pizza. (p80)

Ramen Tatsu-ya Get your spicy ramen fix here. (p79)

Tacodeli Taco perfection made sublime by the spicy dona sauce. (p79)

SAMYSTCLAIR/GETTY IMAGES ©

Best Old Favorites

Güero's Taco Bar Everybody loves Güero's for the tacos, margaritas and conviviality. (p81)

Texas Chili Parlor Load up your chili with cheese and sour cream. (p43)

Fonda San Miguel Old Mexico dishes drawing fans for 25 years. (p110)

Kerbey Lane Café Great service, big menu, delicious food – a winner. (p108)

Best Evening Out

Uchiko Innovative sushi and Japanese specialties in warmly glossy digs. (p106)

Dai Due Flavor-packed fare from the butcher next door and farms nearby. (p61)

Barley Swine Seasonal farm-to-table specialties and great cocktails. (p109)

Wink Modern French and Asian dishes are ready for your date night. (p109)

Launderette Lauded restaurant serving Mediterranean-inspired meals. (p60)

Worth a Trip

They call it the **Texas Barbecue Trail** (www. texasbbqtrails.com): 80 artery-clogging miles of the best brisket, ribs and sausage Texas has to offer, stretching from Taylor (36 miles northeast of Austin) down to Luling. Marketing gimmick? Perhaps. Do our stomachs care? They do not. If your schedule or limited appetite make driving two hours and eating at 12 different barbecue restaurants unfeasible, make a beeline for brisket in Lockhart, or, if it's hot sausage you crave, Elgin is your best bet.

Bar Open

There are bajillions of bars in Austin. The legendary 6th St bar scene has spilled onto nearby thoroughfares, especially Red River St. Many 6th St places are shot bars aimed at college students and tourists. The Red River establishments retain a harder local edge. A few blocks south, Rainey St is also jumping, with old bungalows now home to watering holes. The coffee culture is strong.

6th Street

Sixth St cuts across the city. In and around downtown, sections of the street have different nicknames when it comes to nightlife. Dirty 6th is the wild, bar-lined section stretching from Congress Ave east to I-35. East 6th refers to the burgeoning strip of restaurants and bars lining 6th St east of I-35 in East Austin. West 6th, west of Congress Ave, has a few solid dive bars and live-music venues. Also note that 6th St runs one way, from east to west, between Hwy 1/MoPac Expwy and I-35.

Chicken Shit Bingo

We love the Little Longhorn Saloon (p110) any old time, but for a uniquely Austin outing, you've really got to experience the Sunday-night phenomenon known as Chicken Shit Bingo. Beer-swilling patrons throw down their bets of $2 per square and wait to see what number the chicken 'chooses,' with the whole pot going to the winner. The chicken doesn't seem to mind.

Coffee Culture

Austin's a laid-back kind of town, so cultivate your slacker vibe by hanging out, sipping coffee and watching everyone else doing the same. Most places offer light meals too.

Best Coffee Culture

Bouldin Creek Coffee House Very representative of the South Austin scene, with a great vegetarian menu to boot. (p79)

Hideout Coffee House & Theatre Despite its downtown location, it has a near-campus vibe and damn fine brews. (p47)

KUMAR SRISKANDAN/ALAMY STOCK PHOTO ©

Sa-Ten Coffee & Eats Enjoy Japanese snacks with your latte in an East Austin artists complex. (p63)

Mozart's Coffee Roasters On Lake Austin you'll find a great waterfront view and a sinful dessert case. (p124)

Spider House North of campus, Spider House has a big patio bedecked with all sorts of oddities. It's open late and also serves beer and wine. (p98)

Best Craft Beer

Easy Tiger Laid-back beer garden between a creek and a bakery. (p45)

Craft Pride On Rainey St, only sells Texas beers. (p46)

ABGB Picnic tables, live music, great home brews and tasty pizza. (p82)

Scholz Garten Long-running downtown favorite with beers and barbecue. (p98)

Jester King Brewery In Dripping Springs, serving sour beers in a rustic setting. (p122)

Best Atmosphere

Driskill Hotel With taxidermy and leather couches, this clubby bar is prime for making deals. (p46)

Mean Eyed Cat The whole interior is an ode to Johnny Cash. (p110)

Hotel San José Hip style and fine drinks in a South Austin courtyard. (p82)

Whisler's If Austin has vampires, they surely lurk in this dark cocktail bar. (p62)

Garage Craft cocktails in a parking garage hideaway. (p46)

Top Tip: Food Trucks at Bars

Some of the best late-night bars don't serve food but you can recharge at food trucks permanently parked on the property, usually in the yard out back. Check the bar's website before heading out if you think you might get late-night munchies.

Showtime

When it comes to the performing arts, there is more to Austin than live music. The city is home to a thriving movie-going culture, an active local theater community and a strong comedy and improv scene. And college-football viewing at UT is no small affair, with average attendance per game topping 95,000.

Find a Perfomance

Entertainment information can be found in the *Austin Chronicle*, out on Thursdays, or on the *Austin American-Statesman's* 360 website (www.austin360.com). The latter has streamlined listings for concerts and nightlife. The *Chronicle's* night-by-night encyclopedia of listings often includes set times, plus music critics' picks and local gossip.

Live Music

On any given Friday night there are several hundred acts playing, and even on a Monday or Tuesday, you'll typically have your pick of performances. Cover charges range from $5 for local bands to $15 or more for touring acts. Music shows often start late and doors almost always open half an hour to an hour before show-time. Showing up at the last minute or fashionably late may result in not getting in. If you want to start early, most places have a happy hour (4pm to 7pm).

Spectator Sports

The whole town turns burnt orange during University of Texas game weekends. (Longhorn fans are probably not flipping you off: it's just the two-fingered sign for 'Hook 'em Horns.') For tickets to any university-sponsored sporting event, contact the UT box office (p93).

MACH PHOTOS/SHUTTERSTOCK ©

Best Performance Venues

Cactus Cafe Listen to acoustic up close and personal at this intimate club on the UT campus. (p98)

Frank Erwin Center Known as 'The Drum' among UT students, this major venue holds up to 17,000 screaming fans. (p98)

Paramount Theatre This old vaudevillian house dates from 1915. (p48)

Stubb's Bar-B-Q Small indoor stage and a main backyard concert venue. Excellent acoustics. (p47)

Antone's This key player has attracted the best of the blues and other popular local acts since 1975. (p47)

Best Music Festivals

South by Southwest (SXSW) One of America's biggest and most varied music-industry gatherings. (www.sxsw.com; single festival $825-1325, combo pass $1150-1650; ☉mid-Mar)

Austin City Limits Three-day autumn festival, held in Zilker Park. (www.aclfestival.com; 1-/3-day pass $100/225; ☉Oct)

Best Live-Music Venues in South Austin

Continental Club Legendary 1950s-era lounge with a swingin' dance floor. (p83)

Saxon Pub Relaxed rock- and blues-oriented venue. (p84)

Emo's East Standout venue hosting punk, rock and more. (p84)

Stubb's Bar-B-Q Multiple stages and live music almost every night. (p47)

Best Dance Halls

Broken Spoke Perhaps *the* authentic Texas honky-tonk in Austin. (p83)

Mercer Street Dance Hall Live country music, two-stepping and ice-cold beer. (p127)

White Horse Diverse and friendly honky-tonk. (p62)

Treasure Hunt

SIMON LEIGH/ALAMY STOCK PHOTO ©

Not many folks visit Austin just to shop, but there are enough home-grown indie shops with unique finds that it's worth setting aside a few hours to check out what's on offer.

Record Shops

Music is a huge industry here and you'll find heaps of it in Austin's record stores. The best stores let you listen to just about anything before you buy, and will carry the bands you see around town.

Vintage Apparel & Furnishings

Vintage is a lifestyle, and the city's best hunting grounds for retro fashions and furnishings are South Austin and Guadalupe St near UT. For more vintage-fashion options, check out www.vintagearound townguide.com.

Best Arts & Antiques

Uncommon Objects Eclectic assortment of antiques on S Congress Ave. (p73)

Austin Art Garage Works from local artists with distinctive style. (p84)

Mexic-Arte Museum Fantastic Mexican crafts for sale in the gift shop. (p42)

Yard Dog Folk art with lots of personality is the draw at this South Congress gallery. (p85)

Tesoros Trading Co Colorful collection of folk art, much of it from Latin America. (p73)

Best Indie Shops

Allens Boots Cowboy boots by various makers fill the aisles. (p73)

BookPeople Inc Huge indie bookstore with author readings and great staff recommendations. (p103)

Waterloo Records Amazing vinyl selection and welcoming staff. (p103)

Big Top Candy Shop Old-fashioned candy, gummy bears and ice cream. What's not to love? (pictured; p73)

Toy Joy So many toys, so little time. (p49)

Outdoor Activities

Austin has numerous places to play outside, including Zilker Park, Lady Bird Lake, and creekside parks and green-belts. You can get just about any information you might need from the City of Austin Parks & Recreation Department (www.austintexas.gov/department/parks-and-recreation). Check the website for everything from municipal golf courses to tennis complexes.

T ATKINS/500PX ©

Cycling & Hiking

With 10 miles of trails looping around Lady Bird Lake, the Ann & Roy Butler Hike-and-Bike Trail & Boardwalk (p76) is a popular spot for exercise. The trail runs most of the way along the lake's northern side, which is the south edge of downtown Austin, and along the lake's southern side, buffering South Austin. You can also hike or mountain bike for almost 8 miles along the Barton Creek Greenbelt (p76), which can be entered near Barton Springs Pool. If you visit the Lady Bird Johnson Wildflower Center, add time to ride or skate the great 3.1-mile Veloway track (p78) nearby. The track runs clockwise, and no walking or running is permitted.

Outdoor Swimming

Austinites escape the heat at local swimming holes (often formed by cold springs). So pack your swimsuit if you're visiting the city in summer (although the pools are open year-round). You'll find popular spring-fed pools in Zilker Park, Dripping Springs and along the Barton Creek Greenbelt. No swimming is allowed in Lady Bird Lake, although you can paddle across it in watercraft.

Best Outdoor Activities

Barton Springs Pool Swim laps in a cold spring-fed pool. (p69)

Lady Bird Lake Rent a kayak and paddle on waters in view of downtown. (p120)

Mt Bonnell Short climb leads to the highest point in the city and Lake Austin views. (p114)

Hamilton Pool Preserve Swim in a lush box canyon pool beneath a waterfall. (p120)

Museums

Most of the city's museums cluster in two places: downtown and the University of Texas (UT) campus. The two art museums downtown are noted for their avant-garde and thoughtful temporary exhibits. In the UT area, museums tackle Texas history, art, natural science and written and photographic artifacts. Offbeat museums are scattered across town.

TERRY HUNTINGDON TYDINGS/SHUTTERSTOCK ©

Best History Museums

Bob Bullock Texas State History Museum A big museum spotlighting the state's big story. (p36)

Lyndon Baines Johnson (LBJ) Library & Museum Covers the background and social programs of the 36th president of the US. (p90)

Texas State Capitol Guided and self-guided tours highlight unique features. (p34)

Harry Ransom Humanities Research Center Spotlights written and photographic treasures. (p93)

George Washington Carver Museum Shares the history of Juneteenth and the stories of prominent Austin African American families. (p56)

Best Art Museums

Blanton Museum of Art Check out the intriguing special exhibits. (p93)

Mexic-Arte Museum Thought-provoking works from Mexican and Mexican American artists. (p42)

Contemporary Austin Up-to-the-minute art downtown, plus a statue garden in West Austin. (p42)

Best Unique Museums

Museum of the Weird Offbeat and mysterious artifacts from around the world. (p42)

Elisabet Ney Museum Statue-filled studio of one of Austin's great sculptors. (pictured; p96)

SouthPop Austin's cultural highlights are covered here. (p77)

Top Tips: Museum Finds

○ Admission to the Bob Bullock Texas State History Museum is free on the first Sunday of the month.

○ The freestanding Capitol Visitors Center has several exhibits about the capitol building.

Under the Radar Austin

ROSCHETZKY PHOTOGRAPHY/SHUTTERSTOCK ©

After you've hit the music bars and explored the culinary creativity of South Congress, head off the beaten path to some of Austin's lesser-known wonders. You'll find architectural oddities, forested reserves and hidden lakes ideal for an afternoon of skinny dipping.

Wild Basin Wilderness Preserve

Located less than a 20-minute drive from Austin, this 227-acre **nature reserve** (www.stedwards.edu/wild-basin) immerses you in the beauty of the Hill Country woodlands. Some 2.5 miles of trails dot the park, with scenic overlooks, creek crossings and a waterfall all part of the backdrop. Keep an eye out for unique plant and animal species including the endangered golden-cheeked warbler.

Twin Falls & Sculpture Falls

It's worth the 3.2-mile round-trip hike from the trailhead near the MoPac Mobility Bridge to see these falls (Twin Falls pictured) tucked into the Barton Creek Greenbelt Trail (p86). They become refreshing swimming holes on hot days.

Casa Neverlandia

Artist and architect **James Talbot** (www.facebook.com/casaneverlandia) does his part to keep the creative fires of the city burning from his studio in South Austin. Book ahead for a tour, which includes fire poles between floors, secret passages and a look-out tower accessed by a rickety bridge.

Hippie Hollow

The only clothing-optional **public park** (www.parks.traviscounty tx.gov/parks/hippie-hollow) in Texas is a mere 30-minute drive northwest of Austin. The big draw is a swim in the sparkling waters of Lake Travis, followed by a bit of tan-line-free sunning on the rocky shoreline. Don't bring the kids, as it's strictly 18 and over.

Weird Austin

For years, Austin's unofficial motto has been 'Keep Austin Weird.' Bumper stickers and T-shirts insist upon it, but are they succeeding? Check out www.keepaustinweird.com to find out what's odd right now.

DOLLAR TRAVELERS/SHUTTERSTOCK ©

History of Weird

When asked why he was a making a donation to *The Lounge Show,* a radio program that played unusual songs, back in 2002, Austin Community College librarian Red Wassenich said he wanted to 'Keep Austin Weird.' His wish soon became a rallying cry as the cheap and offbeat city became more corporate with all the new arrivals. Wassenich and his wife subsequently printed Keep Austin Weird bumper stickers, and he penned a book spotlighting the city's weirdest attractions. Today, ever-growing bedroom community Dripping Springs dubs itself West of Weird.

Best Weird Sights

Cathedral of Junk A climbable backyard sculpture that turns discarded items into art. (pictured; p77)

Museum of the Weird Animal deformities, shrunken heads and a live show! (p42)

Alamo Drafthouse Cinema Home to Master Pancake Theater and other offbeat events. (p47)

Little Longhorn Saloon Chicken Shit Bingo in this dive bar. (p110)

Christmas lights 37th St east of Lamar lights up in December.

Murals Eclectic artworks are scattered across the city.

Best Annual Events

Eeyore's Birthday Party An annualfestival where weirdness reigns supreme. (p111)

Austin Hot Sauce Festival Fiery sauces are feted in a hot month – August!

Bat Fest August festival honoring the city's Mexican free-tailed bats.

For Free

STEPHANIEFARRELL/SHUTTERSTOCK ©

It's easy to have fun on the cheap in this city, which is filled with starving artists, hardworking musicians and many students. Highlights include the nightly bat migration, murals and outdoor art, city parks and the state capitol complex.

Best Free Sights

Austin Art Garage Offbeat gallery that captures the spirit of Austin's art scene. (p84)

Elisabet Ney Museum Former home of – and now gallery dedicated to – this important sculptor. (p96)

Texas State Capitol This state capitol, built from sunset-red granite, is the largest in the US. Free tours too. (p34)

Mayfield House & Nature Preserve Look for the peacocks (pictured) and stroll along the river. (p120)

Best Murals & Graffiti

Greetings from Austin This colorful postcard will brighten any Instagram feed. (p76)

I Love You So Much Couples pose before this simple declaration of affection. (p76)

Hi, How Are You Kurt Cobain wore a T-shirt adorned with this very frog. (p96)

Hope Outdoor Gallery This arts nonprofit's famous graffiti site closed in 2019; at time of writing, a new park near the airport was due to open in 2022. (www.hopeoutdoorgallery.com)

Top Tips: Find Out More

○ For more recommendations about free stuff to do in Austin, visit www.freefunin austin.com.

○ Find free daily concerts and performances listed at www.do512.com/free.

LGBTIQ+ Austin

BIBRAK QAMAR CHANDIO/SHUTTERSTOCK ©

With a thriving gay population – not to mention pretty mellow straight people – Austin is arguably the most gay-friendly city in Texas. Businesses and bars are typically welcoming across the city. The bar and club scene is centered in the Warehouse District downtown, particularly along W 4th St between Lavaca and Colorado Sts.

Resources

The **Austin Gay & Lesbian Chamber of Commerce** (3007 N Lamar Blvd; www. aglcc.org) sponsors the Pride Parade (pictured) in August, as well as smaller events throughout the year. It also compiles a helpful online directory of gay-owned and -friendly businesses. For music and media-related events, visit www.Republiq.com. The *Austin Chronicle* (www.austinchronicle. com) runs the Gay Place, a gay event column. Radio station 97.5 Pride Radio (www.975pride.iheart. com) programs music for LGBTIQ+ listeners and friends.

Around Texas

Arguably the most welcoming city in all Texas for gay, lesbian, bisexual and transgender travelers, and home to one of the state's largest Pride events, Austin has long been embraced by LGBTIQ+ visitors as a home from home.

Best LGBTIQ+ Bars

Oilcan Harry's Dance club for the boys. (p46)

Rain on 4th Dance club with weekly events. (217 W 4th St; www.rainon4th.com)

Highland Lounge Get your sexy on with cocktails and dancing. There's a patio too. (404 Colorado St; www. highlandlounge.com)

Cheer Up Charlies Sip beer, wine and kombucha on the covered patio. (900 Red River St; www.cheerup charlies.com)

For Kids

Austin is kid-friendly, thanks to the casual south-central Texas lifestyle. Zilker Park (p68) is always a good bet for outdoor fun, with loads of indoor and outdoor options.

BRANDON SEIDEL/SHUTTERSTOCK ©

Necessities

Dining It's more than fine to bring kids along to casual restaurants, which often have high chairs and children's menus.

Lodging Most motels and hotels offer rooms with two double beds, and some have roll-away beds or cribs that can be brought into the room for an extra charge. Some hotels offer 'kids stay free' programs for children up to 18 years old. Most B&Bs do not allow children under 12 to stay.

Supplies Baby food, formula, soy and cow's milk, disposable diapers (nappies) and other necessities are widely available in drugstores and supermarkets. Breastfeeding in public is accepted when done dis-

creetly. Many public toilets have a baby-changing table, and gender-neutral 'family' bathrooms may be available at airports, museums etc.

Best for Children

Zilker Zephyr Ride around Zilker Park on a miniature train. (pictured; p87)

Austin Nature & Science Center Exhibits about Texas flora and fauna, plus trails in Zilker Park. (p69)

Barton Springs Pool Cool off in this ginormous natural pool with icy-cold water. (p69)

Thinkery Huge museum with hands-on science, technology and arts activities. (p56)

Texas Memorial Museum Dinosaurs on the UT campus. (p96)

Mayfield House & Nature Preserve Peacocks and trails. (p120)

Top Tip: Storytime

Mix your book-shopping with a children's storytime gathering on Saturdays at 11:30am at BookPeople Inc (p103).

Four Perfect Days

Day One

Start your day with gingerbread pancakes at **Kerbey Lane Café** (p108) then head to the **Bob Bullock Texas State History Museum** (p36), where the *Austin City Limits* exhibit sets an upbeat mood for exploring. Pop in to the **Blanton Museum of Art** (pictured; p93) across the street for eye-catching art.

Stroll Guadalupe St in search of lunch and swing by the **Hi, How Are You mural** (p96) and its smile from Jeremiah the Frog. In the afternoon, cool off at **Barton Springs Pool** (p69), before Tex-Mex at **Trudy's Texas Star** (p97).

After dark, sit on the patio with sandwiches and beers at **Easy Tiger** (p45). Finally, plug into Austin's live-music scene with some club-hopping along Red River or in the Warehouse District.

Day Two

On day two, explore the **Texas State Capitol** (p34), starting inside with a free guided tour. Don't miss the towering dome over the rotunda.

Head to South Congress Ave for lunch at **Güero's Taco Bar** (p81), followed by boot shopping at **Allens Boots** (p73) and old-fashioned candy at **Big Top Candy Shop** (p73). Take a selfie beside the **I Love You So Much mural** (p76) then settle in at a table on a sidewalk patio for people-watching. Stroll Lady Bird Lake on the **Ann & Roy Butler Hike-and-Bike Trail & Boardwalk** (p76).

If it's summer, go to the Congress Avenue Bridge to witness the nightly exodus of America's largest urban **bat colony** (p66). End your evening with Texas two-stepping at **Broken Spoke** (pictured; p83).

Day Three

JORDAN SCHAEFER/SHUTTERSTOCK ©

On day three, road-trip to Dripping Springs, known as the Gateway to the Hill Country, 25 miles west of Austin. Jump into the refreshing swimming hole at **Hamilton Pool Preserve** (pictured; p120), which is tucked in a green wonderland. Reservations are often required so check before you leave.

Grab barbecue at **Salt Lick** (p121) or pizza at **Pieous** (p121). Spend the afternoon visiting wineries, microbreweries and distilleries, followed by a stroll though the historic downtown and a cup of coffee at **Mazama Coffee Co** (p127).

In the evening, forget your calorie counting with gourmet Southern comfort food at **Homespun** (p127). Enjoy an after-dinner beer at the **Barber Shop** (p127) or **Mercer Street Dance Hall** (p127).

Day Four

PHILIP ARNO PHOTOGRAPHY/SHUTTERSTOCK ©

The next day, check out a couple of the smaller museums around town. On the UT campus, find the bones of a Cretaceous-era flying reptile at the **Texas Memorial Museum** (p96) and loads of information about a former president at the **Lyndon Baines Johnson (LBJ) Library & Museum** (p90). A rare Gutenberg Bible is displayed at the **Ransom Center** (p93).

After lunch at one of the city's many barbecue joints, enjoy some outdoor time by hiking up to the summit of **Mount Bonnell** (p114), or strolling through the flowers and plant life at the **Lady Bird Johnson Wildflower Center** (pictured; p70).

Make dinner a moveable feast by roaming the food trucks. End with a live show at the **Continental Club** (p83).

Need to Know

For detailed information, see Survival Guide (p145)

Currency
US dollar ($)

Time
Central Time Zone
(GMT/UTC -5)

Visas
Visitors from many
countries don't need
visas for stays of less
than 90 days, though
must get approval from
the Electronic System
for Travel Authorization
(ESTA). Visitors from
Canada need neither a
visa nor ESTA approval
for short stays. Check
www.travel.state.gov.

Money
Credit cards are widely
accepted and often
required for hotel
reservations and car
rentals. ATMs are easy
to find.

Cell Phones
Prepaid local SIM cards
are widely available.
Reception can be
spotty in rural areas.

Tipping
Tipping is not optional.
Service employees
make minimum wage
and rely on tips.

Daily Budget

Budget: Less than $120
Campground or dorm bed: $10–40
Basic motel room: $60–95
Tacos, pizza or takeout: $2–15
Bus: $3.50

Midrange: $200–300
B&B or better quality motel: $120–195
Cafe meals and food-truck takeout: $6–25
Compact car rental and fuel: $50
Movies, museums and admissions: $15

Top End: More than $350
Upscale hotel: $300–655
Restaurant meals and fine dining: from $30
Intermediate to luxury car rental and fuel: $50–95
Museums, shows, major attractions, theme parks: $30–55

Advance Planning

Plan well ahead for South by Southwest
(SXSW). The most affordable option is to buy
early-bird tickets before mid-September. The
price increases approximately $100 per month
after that until showtime. Hotel rooms fill
months ahead of time.

Arriving in Austin

✈ Austin-Bergstrom International Airport

Around 30 minutes southeast of downtown.

Taxi Cost around $30 to downtown.

Bus Capital Metro bus 20 connects the airport with downtown for just $1.25, with departures every 15 minutes.

Car You can walk from the terminal to the rental car facility. All major rental car agencies are represented.

Rideshare A typical ride between the airport and downtown costs around $22.

Getting Around

You can explore several communities by foot: downtown, the Market District, S Congress Ave in South Austin, E 6th St in East Austin and the University of Texas. However, you will need to drive or catch a bus between most of these. You can also walk to Lady Bird Lake from downtown and S Congress Ave.

🚗 Car

Useful for exploring several neighborhoods and for day trips to Dripping Springs and Lockhart. Downtown street parking is metered. Elsewhere parking is free but check signage for permit and time limit requirements.

🚌 Bus

Regular **Capital Metro** (CapMetro; ☎512-474-1200, transit store 512-389-7454; www.capmetro.org; ⏰transit store 7:30am-5:30pm Mon-Fri) buses – not including the more expensive express routes – cost $1.25. Children under six are free. Almost all CapMetro buses, including more than a dozen UT shuttle routes, have bicycle racks on the front.

🚲 Bicycle

The city has more than 40 Austin B-cycle (www.austin.bcycle.com) bike-sharing stations.

🚗 Rideshare & Taxi

Both Uber (www.uber.com) and Lyft (www.lyft.com) operate here.

You'll usually need to call and request a cab, rather than flagging one on the street. Larger companies include **Yellow Cab** (☎512-452-9999) and **Austin Cab** (☎512-478-2222).

Austin Neighborhoods

West Austin (p113)
Drive west for views and jaunts into nature, followed by easy conviviality at microbreweries, distilleries and wineries.

Mt Bonnell

Market District, Clarksville & North Austin (p101)
Close to downtown, the Market District and Clarksville are made for strolling and shopping. North Austin has good dinner options.

Zilker Park

Dripping Springs (15mi)

South Austin (p65)
Eclectic shops and eateries line S Congress Ave; fun beckons at Zilker Park.

San Antonio (p128)
Historic buildings, some fabulous parks and museums, and a truly cosmopolitan mix of peoples and cultures make up this fast-growing city.

Lady Bird Johnson Wildflower Center

San Antonio (73mi)

UT & Central Austin (p89)
A presidential library, an art museum and tours keep history alive.

University of Texas at Austin ⊙

Lyndon Baines Johnson (LBJ) Library & Museum ⊙

⊙ Bob Bullock Texas State History Museum

⊙ Texas State Capitol

⊙ Bat Colony Under the Congress Avenue Bridge

East Austin (p51)
Dive bars bump elbows with glossy apartments in this evolving area. After work, E 6th St thrums with festivity and food trucks.

Downtown Austin (p33)
Buttoned up by day, downtown offers shooters, bands and beers by night.

Explore
Austin

Austin's Walking Tours

View along Congress Ave towards Texas State Capitol TOD GRUBBS/500PX ©

Explore ⊕

Downtown Austin

Downtown is the hardworking hub of the city, home to the state capitol complex, several museums and numerous hotels catering to politicians, business travelers and convention-goers. Downtown plays hard, too. The neighborhood is chock-full of entertainment options, including the wild shot bars of 6th St, the more low-key bars of Rainey St and music venues in Red River.

The Short List

○ **Texas State Capitol (p34)** *Touring the country's largest state capitol.*

○ **Bob Bullock Texas State History Museum (p36)** *Learning the story of beloved hero and city namesake Stephen Austin.*

○ **Stubb's Bar-B-Q (p47)** *Chowing down on brisket then catching a live show at one of the city's most beloved music venues.*

○ **Alamo Drafthouse Cinema (p47)** *Talking back to the screen during an event night at Austin's home-grown movie theater.*

○ **Easy Tiger (p45)** *Sipping a Texas craft brew at a lovely local beer garden.*

Getting There & Around

🚌 Capital Metro routes between 1 and 99 connect with downtown. The 100 Airport Flyer runs to/from the airport.

🚗 The north–south MoPac Expwy/Hwy Loop 1 borders downtown to the west. I-35 parallels MoPac to the east.

🚉 The Texas Eagle stops at the Amtrak station just west of downtown.

Downtown Austin Map on p40

6th St ARPAD BENEDEK/GETTY IMAGES ©

Top Experience 📷
See Government in Action at Texas State Capitol

Built in 1888 from sunset-red granite, this state capitol is the largest in the US, backing up the ubiquitous claim that everything is bigger in Texas. If nothing else, take a peek at the lovely rotunda – be sure to look up at the dome – and try out the whispering gallery created by its curved ceiling.

◎ MAP P40, D3

✎ tours 512-305-8402

cnr 11th St & Congress Ave

admission free

🕐 7am-10pm Mon-Fri, 9am-8pm Sat & Sun

South Foyer

Loaded with sculptures and artwork, the South Foyer is an inspiring place to begin your trip through the capitol building. It's also the starting point for guided tours. Statues of local heroes Stephen F Austin and Sam Houston stand nobly beside the entrance to the rotunda. Both were carved by artist Elisabet Ney and presented in 1903. Alamo fighter Davy Crockett is honored in a grand painting by Texas artist William Henry Huddle. Crockett's portrait adorns the wall across from an equally grand painting of the *Surrender of Santa Anna*, also painted by Huddle. African American politicians serving the state prior to 1900 are shown in a composite beside the rotunda.

The Rotunda & Dome

It's hard to know which way to look when entering the massive rotunda on the first level. There's an eye-catching feature in every direction. On the floor, the seals of the six countries whose flags have flown over Texas surround the Great Seal. Six?! Yep. Spain, France, Mexico, the Republic of Texas (a country from 1836 to 1845), the Confederate States of America and the US. The star in the dome overhead is 218ft above you and the seemingly tiny star actually stretches 8ft across from point to point.

Legislative Chambers

Texas history comes to life in two massive paintings adorning the back wall of the Senate chamber: the clash at the Alamo and the battle of San Jacinto. Thirty-one state senators meet in this 2nd-story chamber. The 150 members of the House of Representatives meet across the rotunda in a separate chamber. To see the government in action, take a seat in the 3rd-floor visitor balconies overlooking the House of Representatives and Senate chamber galleries, which are open to the public when the state legislature is in session (odd-numbered years from mid-January through May or June).

★ Top Tips

∘ Free two-hour parking is available inside the Capitol Visitors Parking Garage, entered from either 12th St or 13th St, off San Jacinto Blvd.

∘ You'll find an exhibit about the building in the freestanding visitor center on the southeast corner of the grounds.

∘ Self-guided-tour brochures of the building and grounds are available inside the tour guide office on the ground floor. From here you can also take an interesting 40-minute guided tour (periodically 8:30am to 4:30pm Monday to Friday, 9:30am to 3:30pm Saturday, noon to 3:30pm Sunday). The green sprawl of the capitol grounds and its monuments are worth a stroll.

✕ Take a Break

Enjoy lunch at longtime favorite the Texas Chili Parlor (p43).

For a caffeine pick-me-up, walk south to Hideout Coffee House & Theatre (p47).

Top Experience 📷
Remember the Alamo at Bob Bullock Texas State History Museum

This is no dusty historical museum. Big and glitzy, it shows off the Lone Star State's history, from when it used to be part of Mexico up to the present, with high-tech interactive exhibits and fun theatrics.

◎ MAP P40, D1

📞 512-936-8746

www.thestoryoftexas.com

1800 Congress Ave

adult/child $13/9

🕘 9am-5pm Mon-Sat, noon-5pm Sun

La Belle: The Ship That Changed History

A permanent exhibit on the 1st floor showcases the history – and the recovered hull – of *La Belle*, a French ship that sank off the Gulf Coast in the 1680s, changing the course of Texas history. Exhibits explore the ship's remarkable story: sent by King Louis XIV of France under the command of René-Robert Cavelier, Sieur de la Salle, *La Belle* was one of four vessels carrying 400 passengers to the new world, where they were to establish a colony and trade routes. All four ships were eventually lost, with *La Belle* sinking off the Texas coast in 1686. Archaeologists have recovered 1.4 million artifacts; muskets, glass beads and farming tools are on display.

Story of Texas

The Texas History galleries are the core of the museum, and more than 700 artifacts are displayed across three floors. The 1st floor focuses on *La Belle,* while exhibits on the 2nd floor trace Texas history from 1821 to 1936. A statue of Texas statesman and hero Sam Houston marks the entrance. As you explore, you'll discover more about Texas booster Stephen F Austin (check out his pine desk) and learn more about the Alamo, Texas Comanches and the lives of African Americans. Oil and cattle exhibits are highlights on the 3rd floor while the *Austin City Limits* display livens up the scene with music.

IMAX & the Star of Destiny

The museum also houses Austin's first IMAX theater (check website for listings; adult/child 4-17yr $9/7) and the Texas Spirit Theater (adult/child 4-17yr $5/4). Both offer discounted combination tickets when bought with a museum admission. The Texas Spirit Theater is where you can see *The Star of Destiny,* a 15-minute special-effects film that's simultaneously high-tech and hokey fun.

★ Top Tips

○ Don't waste too much time driving around looking for parking. The lot beneath the building is convenient and costs a flat $8.

○ The always compelling Blanton Museum of Art (p93) is across the street, so save an extra hour to check it out.

✗ Take a Break

If all that history has you craving Tex-Mex and a margarita, don't worry, Trudy's Texas Star (p97) has you covered. You could also grab a beer at Scholz Garten (p98).

Walking Tour 🚶

Downtown: Politics & Culture

Downtown is a lively jumble of politicians, office workers, tourists, creatives and a fair number of homeless folks. Cops on bikes patrol the area, particularly near gritty 6th St, but generally the streets are safe. Lined with historic buildings, art museums and cool cafes, Congress Ave is the main thoroughfare, and it's an invigorating place to stroll.

Walk Facts
Start Texas State Capitol
End Mexic-Arte Museum
Length 1 mile; 30 minutes

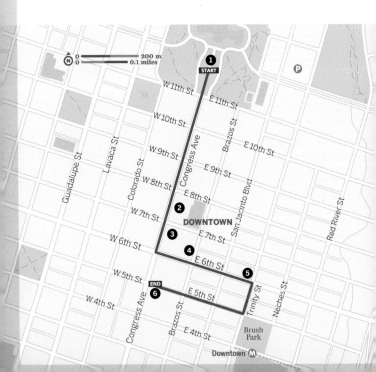

❶ Capitol Grounds

Crowds can be distracting in the **state capitol building** (p34), but the sprawling grounds are typically tranquil. Here, an easy, tree-lined walk passes 20 statues and memorials. On the south lawn look for the Texas cowboy and a monument honoring heroes of the Alamo. The Tejano Monument spotlights the contributions of Spanish and Mexican settlers to the state's history and culture.

❷ Congress Avenue

Austin was established in 1839 to serve as the capital of the Republic of Texas. Development plans called for a 120ft-wide ceremonial boulevard stretching from the capitol to the Colorado River. No buildings from that era survive, but the grand boulevard – Congress Ave – still thrives. Today, buildings date from various eras. The **Paramount Theatre** (p48) celebrated its 100th anniversary in 2015.

❸ Caffeine Fix

Scruffy and crowded, **Hideout Coffee House** (p47) stands apart from the competition because of the small improv theater in the back. Step in for a latte, a pastry and maybe some audience participation.

❹ Driskill Bar

This **clubby place** (p46) feels like Texas. There's a longhorn steer mounted over the fireplace, a copper tin ceiling overhead and cowhide covers on the chairs. And lots of private areas to loosen your tie or kick off your heels. Join politicians, screenwriters, musicians and everyone else in search of a good cocktail in a bar that knows what it's doing.

❺ Movie Lovers Unite

Cinephiles flock to **Alamo Drafthouse** (p47) for food, beer and a great movie-going experience. Think comfy seats and absolutely no tolerance for talking or cell phone use. An Austin original, Alamo Drafthouses are now scattered across the state and venturing into non-Texas territory. Check the online calendar (the Ritz location) for dance parties, Girlie Night (watch *The Notebook*!) and Terror Tuesday flicks.

❻ Mexic-Arte Museum

The exhibits rotate regularly at this airy contemporary **museum** (p42), so popping in always feels like a mini-adventure. Even better, it's a small place, so you can immerse in the art – which spotlights Mexican and Latino works – and never feel rushed. If you're looking for a unique present, the gift shop is loaded with eclectic arts and crafts.

Downtown Austin

40

JUDGE'S HILL

Charles Forest

House Park

Duncan Park

Shoal Creek

N Lamar Blvd

West Ave

W 17th St
W 16th St
W 15th St
W 14th St
W 13th St
W 12th St
W 11th St
W 10th St
W 9th St
W 8th St
W 7th St
W 6th St

Rio Grande St
Nueces St
San Antonio St
Guadalupe St
Lavaca St
Colorado St
N Congress Ave
Brazos St
San Jacinto Blvd

Bob Bullock State Texas State History Museum ○

Texas State Capitol ★

Texas Governor's Mansion

Wooldridge Square

Faulk Central Library

Contemporary 4 ○
Austin
✪20

DOWNTOWN

Frank C. Erwin Jr. Special Events Center

University Medical Center Brackenridge

Red River St
Trinity St
San Jacinto Blvd
E 18th St
E 17th St
E 16th St
E 15th St
E 14th St
E 13th St
E 12th St
E 11th St
E 10th St
E 9th St
E 8th St

Waterloo Park
Waller Creek

Capitol Visitors Parking Garage Ⓟ

✪25

Sabine St
Red River St
Trinity St

✗6

E Martin Luther King Jr Blvd

500 m
0.25 miles

Downtown Austin

E 7th St
E 6th St
E 5th St
E 4th St
E 3rd St
E 2nd St
E Cesar Chavez St (E 1st St)
Willow St
Spence St
San Marcos St

Interregional Hwy

E 8th St
★17
Neches St
E 7th St
Sabine St
3 Museum of the Weird
E 7th St
23 ★21
14

NIH 35 Frontage Rd
11
Downtown Walking Tours
2
★9
Brushy St
290
35
Palm Park
Red River St
Driskill St
S IH 35 Frontage Rd
Davis St
River St
Rainey St
★12

E 7th St
★19
The Firehouse Hostel
E 6th St
Brazos St
★18
Brush Park
E 5th St
Downtown
Trinity St
Austin Convention Center
Driskill St

★16
The Driskill
DOWNTOWN
★1
Mexic-Arte Museum
24 ★7
Congress Ave
★13
E 4th St
E 3rd St
E 2nd St
E Cesar Chavez St (E 1st St)

W 6th St
22 ★
15
Colorado St
Congress Ave Bridge
S Congress Ave

W 5th St
Republic Square
Guadalupe St
8
10 26
WAREHOUSE DISTRICT
W Cesar Chavez St (W 1st St)
W 3rd St
W 2nd St
S 1st St
Lady Bird Lake

Shoal Creek Greenbelt
★5
Mellow Johnny's Bike Shop
San Antonio St
W 4th St
Ann & Roy Butler Hike-and-Bike Trail
Vic Mathias Shores

W Riverside Dr

5
6
7
8
A
B
C
D
E
F

Sights

Mexic-Arte Museum

MUSEUM

1 MAP P40, C5

This wonderful, eclectic downtown museum features works from Mexican and Mexican American artists in exhibitions that change every two months. Many are drawn from the permanent collection, which includes carved wooden masks, modern Latin American paintings, historic photographs and contemporary art. Don't miss the new and experimental talent on show in the back gallery. (☎512-480-9373; www.mexic-artemuseum.org; 419 Congress Ave; adult/child under 12yr/student $7/1/4, free Sun; ⊙10am-6pm Mon-Thu, to 5pm Fri & Sat, noon-5pm Sun, closed during SXSW)

Moonlight Towers

Keep an eye out for Austin's moonlight towers. All the rage in the late 1800s, these 165ft-tall street lamps were designed to give off the light of a full moon. Austin is the only city in which these historic triangular metal towers topped by a halo of six large bulbs still operate. There are 17 of them remaining around the city: how many can you spot?

Downtown Walking Tours

WALKING

2 MAP P40, E6

The Austin Visitor Center (p153) runs a program of three downtown walking tours. Each lasts 1½ hours, costs $10, and starts either from the capitol steps or the visitor center itself, nearby. Check schedules online, and reserve 48 hours in advance if possible. (☎512-478-0098; www.austintexas.org; 602 E 4th St; $10; ⊙schedules vary)

Museum of the Weird

MUSEUM

3 MAP P40, D5

Pay the entrance fee in the gift shop, then step inside Austin's version of a cabinet of curiosities. It's more of a hallway of curiosities, really, lined with shrunken heads, malformed mammals and other unusual artifacts. The show stealer? The legendary Minnesota Ice Man – is that a frozen prehistoric man under all that ice? See for yourself, then grab a seat for a live show of amazing physical derring-do. (☎512-476-5493; www.museumoftheweird.com; 412 E 6th St; adult/child $12/8; ⊙10am-midnight)

Contemporary Austin

MUSEUM

4 MAP P40, C4

This museum operates two separate sites. The Jones Center, downtown, features rotating exhibits representing new artists,

ERICA DEMPSEY/SHUTTERSTOCK © ARCHITECT: PAUL LEWIS

Jones Center, Contemporary Austin

spreading through two gallery floors plus the two-tier Moody Rooftop, an open-air event space with great city views. The Laguna Gloria (p120) is a 1916 Italianate villa on the shores of Lake Austin that holds temporary exhibits plus an engaging sculpture park. (📞512-453-5312; www.thecontemporaryaustin.org; 700 Congress Ave; adult/child $10/free; ⏰Jones Center 11am-7pm Tue-Sat, noon-5pm Sun, Laguna Gloria 10am-4pm Tue-Sun)

Mellow Johnny's Bike Shop

CYCLING

5 ◉ MAP P40, B5

Say what you will about Lance Armstrong, you can still count on him to find you a pretty good bike. Located right downtown,

Mellow Johnny's is co-owned by the disgraced seven-time Tour de France winner. It rents high-performance bikes as well as commuter bikes, and offers free guided bike rides; check the website for a schedule. (📞512-473-0222; www.mellowjohnnys.com; 400 Nueces St; day use $20-50; ⏰7am-7pm Mon-Fri, 7am-6pm Sat, 8am-5pm Sun)

Eating

Texas Chili Parlor

TEX-MEX $

6 ✖ MAP P40, D2

Ready for an X-rated meal? Venture into the large dining room that lurks behind the frankly unenticing facade of this Austin institution. When ordering your chili, keep in mind that 'X' is mild, 'XX' is spicy and 'XXX' is melt-your-face-off hot. Of course there's more than just chili here; there's Frito pie, which is chili over Fritos. (☏512-472-2828; 1409 Lavaca St; mains $4-10; ⊙11am-2am Mon-Sat, to 1am Sun)

Cooper's Old Time Pit Bar-B-Que

BARBECUE $$

7 ⊗ MAP P40, C6

The downtown lunch crowd has discovered this outpost of beloved Cooper's Bar-B-Que in Llano. Pick your meat at the counter (paid by the pound) then add sides. We're partial to the jalapeño mac-and-cheese, which you won't want to share. The baked beans and the white bread are always free. (☏512-474-2145; www.coopersbbqaustin.com; 217 Congress Ave; beef ribs & brisket per lb $18, other meats vary; ⊙11am-10pm)

Getting Oriented

Downtown Austin is an orderly grid. The main north–south artery is Congress Ave, with Cesar Chavez St running east–west. Most downtown streets are one way, including 6th St, a major westbound thoroughfare, and southbound Guadalupe St (pronounced *guad*-ah-loop locally, despite what you might have learned in Spanish class).

La Condesa

MEXICAN $$

8 ⊗ MAP P40, B6

Here in slacky Slackerville, decor is often an afterthought, but La Condesa came along and changed all that with an eye-poppingly gorgeous space that's colorful, supermodern and artsy, with a dazzling mural taking up an entire wall. If you find the dinners to be a little spendy, come for brunch (in the $9 to $20 range). (☏512-499-0300; www.lacondesa.com; 400 W 2nd St; lunch $11-14, dinner $10-25; ⊙11:30am-2:30pm Mon-Fri, 11am-3pm Sat & Sun, 5-10pm Sun-Wed, to 11pm Thu-Sat)

Moonshine Patio Bar & Grill

AMERICAN $$

9 ⊗ MAP P40, E6

A remarkable relic from Austin's early days, this historic mid-1850s building now houses a large and deservedly popular restaurant, serving upscale Southern-flavored comfort food like shrimp and grits or chicken-fried steak. Happy hour sees half-price appetizers, and there's a lavish Sunday brunch buffet ($20). Dine indoors or beneath the pecan trees on the patio. (☏512-236-9599; www.moonshinegrill.com; 303 Red River St; dinner mains $14-25; ⊙11am-10pm Mon-Thu, to 11pm Fri & Sat, 9am-2pm & 5-10pm Sun)

History of Austin

Things happened quickly in the early days of Austin. In 1837 – just one year after Texas had won its independence from Mexico – settlers founded the town of Waterloo on the banks of the Colorado River. By 1939 the town had been chosen as the state capital and renamed Austin, after Stephen F Austin, a man who had colonized the area and come to be known as the Father of Texas.

In 1960, the Colorado River was dammed near Austin, creating a lake known as Town Lake. Mayor Roy Johnson and Lady Bird Johnson, wife of former president Lyndon B Johnson, spearheaded efforts to improve the banks of the reservoir, leading the successful charge for new trails and landscaping. The lake was renamed in her honor in 2007.

After improvements in 1980, the Congress Avenue Bridge drew the attention of a colony of 1.5 million Mexican free-tailed bats, who now wow crowds with their nightly feeding migration.

Fast-forward to the 1990s, when the tech industry brought another boom. With a well-educated populace (thanks to all those University of Texas grads who never could quite bear to move away), Austin attracted major tech companies. It wasn't all UT grads fueling the movement: Michael Dell founded his computer company in his dorm room in 1984 and promptly dropped out of UT.

Between tech types, UT students, musicians and politicians, Austin has a near-constant influx of new residents. Things are constantly changing in the capital city, for better or for worse.

Lamberts

BARBECUE $$$

10 MAP P40, B6

Torn between barbecue and fine dining? Lamberts serves intelligent updates of American comfort-food classics – some might call it 'uppity barbecue' – in a historic stone building run by Austin chef Lou Lambert. (📞512-494-1500; www.lambertsaustin.com; 401 W 2nd St; lunch $12-19, dinner $19-42; ⏰11am-2:30pm Mon-Sat, to 2pm Sun, 5:30-10pm Sun-Wed, to 10:30pm Thu-Sat)

Drinking

Easy Tiger

BEER GARDEN

11 MAP P40, E6

The one bar on Dirty 6th that all locals love? Easy Tiger, an inside-outside beer garden overlooking Waller Creek, which welcomes all comers with an upbeat communal vibe. Craft beers like local favorite Electric Jellyfish are listed on the chalkboard, while the artisanal sandwiches use tasty bread from

Bar-Hopping Through History

Two of the city's most interesting bars are tucked inside top-notch lodging options that sit across the street from each other downtown. The Firehouse Lounge inhabits the **Firehouse Hostel** (Map p40, D5; 📞512-201-2522; www.firehousehostel.com; 605 Brazos St; dm $33-35, d $109-139; 🍴❄🛜), which is the city's oldest freestanding fire station, with a facade built in 1885. Enter through the bookcase. The Driskill Bar is a clubby place with wall-mounted longhorns. It's nestled deep inside the **Driskill Hotel** (Map p40, D5; 📞512-439-1234; www.driskillhotel.com; 604 Brazos St; d/ste from $190/280; 🅿🍴❄@🛜🐾), built by a cattle baron in the late 1800s.

the bakery upstairs (7am to 2am). The meat is cooked in-house. (📞512-614-4972; www.easytigeraustin.com; 709 E 6th St; ⏰11am-midnight Sun-Wed, to 2am Thu-Sat)

Craft Pride BAR

12 📍 MAP P40, E8

If it ain't brewed in Texas, then it ain't on tap at this dark and cozy bar, which bursts with Lone Star pride. Yep, from the All Call kolsch to the Yellow Rose IPA, all 54 craft beers served here are produced in Texas. Look for the bar at the southern end of Rainey St. (📞512-428-5571; www.craftprideaustin.com; 61 Rainey St; ⏰4pm-2am Mon-Fri, 1pm-2am Sat, 1pm-1am Sun)

Garage LOUNGE

13 📍 MAP P40, C5

Hidden inside a parking garage, this cozy, dimly lit lounge draws a hip but not overly precious Austin crowd who give high marks to the

first-rate cocktails, handsomely designed space and novel location. (📞512-369-3490; www.garagetx.com; 503 Colorado St; ⏰5pm-2am Mon-Sat)

Casino El Camino BAR

14 📍 MAP P40, E5

With a legendary jukebox and even better burgers, this is the spot for serious drinking and late-night carousing. If it's too dark inside, head for the back patio. (📞512-469-9330; 517 E 6th St; ⏰11:30am-2am)

Oilcan Harry's CLUB

15 📍 MAP P40, C5

Oh, yes, there's dancing. And oh, yes, it's packed. (And how are you supposed to dance with all those people in there?) As much as the girls wish it were a mixed crowd, this scene is all about the boys. Sweaty ones. (📞512-320-8823; 211 W 4th St; ⏰2pm-2am Mon-Fri, noon-2am Sat & Sun)

Hideout Coffee House & Theatre
COFFEE

16 MAP P40, D5

Despite its downtown location, it has a near-campus vibe and damn fine brews. (📞512-476-1313; 617 Congress Ave; 🕐7am-10pm Mon-Wed, to midnight Thu & Fri, 8am-noon Sat, 8am-10pm Sun; 🛜)

Entertainment

Stubb's Bar-B-Q
LIVE MUSIC

17 ⭐ MAP P40, E5

Stubb's puts on live music almost every night, with a great mix of premier local and touring acts from across the musical spectrum. Many warm-weather shows are held out back along Waller Creek. It has two stages: a smaller stage indoors and a larger backyard venue. Every Sunday, there's a gospel brunch at 10:30am and 12:30pm. (📞512-480-8341; www.stubbsaustin.com; 801 Red River St;

🕐11am-10pm Mon-Thu, to 11pm Fri & Sat, 10:30am-9pm Sun)

Antone's
LIVE MUSIC

18 ⭐ MAP P40, D5

A key player in Austin's musical history, Antone's has attracted the best of the blues and other popular local acts since 1975. All ages, all the time. (www.facebook.com/antonesnightclub; 305 E 5th St; 🕐showtimes vary)

Alamo Drafthouse Cinema
CINEMA

19 ⭐ MAP P40, D5

Easily the most fun you can have at the movies: sing along with *Grease*, quote along with *The Princess Bride*, or just enjoy food and drink delivered right to your seat during first-run films. Check the website for other locations. (📞512-861-7020; www.drafthouse.com; 320 E 6th St; tickets $12-13)

Beware of the Goddess

She stood atop the Texas State Capitol for nearly 100 years, a star in one hand, a sword in the other. When the **Goddess of Liberty** was removed from her perch and lowered by helicopter as part of a capitol restoration project in 1985, no one had seen her up close since 1888. And, well, wow. How to put this? She was not a handsome woman.

Not only was she badly weathered, she was drop-dead ugly, with hideously exaggerated features meant to be appreciated from 300ft below. She was also 16ft tall. After making a cast for her replacement, they restored her to her former, er, beauty and dropped her off at the Bob Bullock Texas State History Museum (p36) as a display, meaning you can have a face-to-face with the woman people for decades could only admire from afar.

Paramount Theatre THEATER

20 MAP P40, D4

Dating from 1915, this old vaudevillian house has staged everything from splashy Broadway shows to stand-up comics to classic film screenings. (📞512-474-1221; www.austintheatre.org; 713 Congress Ave; 🕓box office noon-5:30pm Mon-Fri, 2hr before showtime Sat & Sun)

Esther's Follies COMEDY

21 MAP P40, E5

Drawing from current events and pop culture, this long-running satire show has a vaudevillian slant, thanks to musical numbers

Downtown Hangouts 💬

Food and drink Folks have enjoyed a darn fine bowl of spicy beef at the Texas Chili Parlor (p43) since 1976; it's only Texas craft brews at Craft Pride (p46) on Rainey St.

Local shows Laugh with locals at Esther's Follies, the long-running comedy show; catch a night of improv at intimate Hideout Coffee House & Theatre.

Bump elbows with bigwigs Deals might be going down at the clubby and historic Driskill Bar (p45) near the capitol grounds.

and, yep, even a magician. Good, harmless fun. (📞512-320-0198; www.esthersfollies.com; 525 E 6th St; reserved seating/general admission $30/25; 🕓shows 8pm Thu-Sat, plus 10pm Fri & Sat)

Cedar Street Courtyard LIVE MUSIC

22 MAP P40, C5

Forget the dark and crowded club scene; this sophisticated courtyard venue serves martinis along with jazz and swing. (📞512-495-9669; www.cedarstreetaustin.com; 208 W 4th St; 🕓4pm-2am Mon-Fri, from 6pm Sat & Sun)

Flamingo Cantina LIVE MUSIC

23 MAP P40, E5

Called 'the last place with soul on 6th,' Austin's premier reggae joint prides itself on its good rasta vibes and bouncy dance floor. Seat yourself on the carpeted bleachers for good views of the stage. (📞512-494-9336; www.flamingocantina.com; 515 E 6th St)

Elephant Room LIVE MUSIC

24 MAP P40, C6

This intimate, subterranean jazz club has a cool vibe, and live music almost every night. The cover charge stays low, mostly free except on weekends, and there are happy-hour shows at 6pm weekdays. (📞512-473-2279; www.elephantroom.com; 315 Congress Ave; 🕓4pm-2am Mon-Fri, from 8pm Sat & Sun)

KICKSTAND/GETTY IMAGES ©

Driskill Hotel (p46)

Hideout Coffee House & Theatre COMEDY

The hipsters' Hideout (see 17 🚇 Map p40, D5) is a small coffeehouse and theater space that rubs shoulders with the big theaters on Congress Ave. Shows here feature live improv with plenty of audience participation. The box office usually opens half an hour before showtime. (📞512-443-3688; www.hideouttheatre.com; 617 Congress Ave; tickets $5-15; ⏰shows usually Thu-Sun)

Austin Symphony PERFORMING ARTS

25 ⭐ MAP P40, F4

Founded in the early 20th century, the city's oldest performing-arts group plays classical and pop music at numerous venues throughout the city. The main performance season runs from September to April. (📞512-476-6064; www.austinsymphony.org; box office 1101 Red River St; tickets $12-55; ⏰box office 9am-5pm Mon-Thu, to 4pm Fri, noon-5pm Sat performance days only, 2hr before showtime performance days)

Shopping

Toy Joy TOYS

26 🔒 MAP P40, B6

This colorful toy store for grown-ups and big kids is an exuberant repository that's packed floor to ceiling with fun. (📞512-320-0090; www.toyjoy.com; 403 W 2nd St; ⏰10am-9pm)

Explore ◈
East Austin

East Austin is on the rise. Just look at all the construction cranes along gentrifying E 6th St. Old-timers will warn you that east of I-35 is dangerous and to be avoided at night. Although the streets retain a gritty feel, and host their fair share of vagrants, the main thoroughfares feel safe. The neighborhood also has a rich history as an African American community, with roots back to the 19th century.

The Short List

o **Franklin Barbecue (p58)** *Making friends in the line then devouring the tender brisket – two hours later.*

o **White Horse (p62)** *Taking a dance lesson and drinking whiskey on tap at a convivial honky-tonk.*

o **Dai Due (p61)** *Enjoying the rich local flavors of farm-to-table fare during a leisurely breakfast.*

o **Whisler's (p62)** *Savoring a finely crafted cocktail in the dark and sexy confines of Whisler's.*

o **Thinkery (p56)** *Letting the kids wear themselves out on the outdoor climbing nets.*

Getting There & Around

🚗 From downtown, take E 7th St to East Austin, crossing beneath I-35.

🚌 From the Red River District downtown, ride bus 4 to E 7th St near Comal St.

🚈 Take MetroRail 550 east from the Downtown Station (401 E 4th St) to the Plaza Saltillo Station (E 5th St near Comal St).

East Austin Map on p54

Franklin Barbecue (p58) UNIVERSITY OF COLLEGE/SHUTTERSTOCK ©

Walking Tour 🚶

East Austin Nightlife

E 6th St is akin to a Wild West town – right before the politicians moved in to stamp out the fun with their rules and regulations. New residential developments loom over dive bars, craft cocktail bars, worn-out retailers and old houses converted into restaurants. It's a vibrant place to wander at night. In the dives, you'll see more hipsters than hooligans.

Walk Facts

Start Licha's Cantina

End Violet Crown Social Club

Length 1 mile; 30 minutes

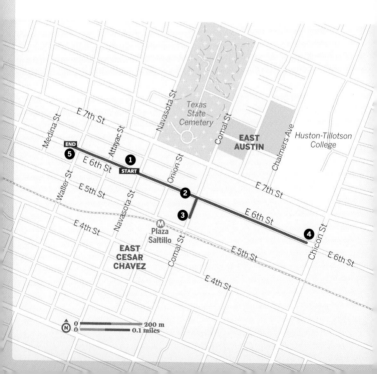

❶ Happy Hour Hot Spot

The bartenders shine at tiny **Licha's Cantina** (p60), a Mexican restaurant spilling out of an old bungalow. It's an upbeat place to fuel up on margaritas, chips and guacamole before heading out. It's also a favorite hole-in-the-wall for locals, so don't tell anyone we told ya about it. Margaritas are $5 from 4pm to 6pm Tuesday to Friday.

❷ Destination: Dive Bar

The strip of E 6th St between Onion and Chicon Sts is packed tight with hip dive bars. It's hard to say if one is better than the other, it just depends on who's there on any particular night. See who's playing at **Hotel Vegas** (1502 E 6th St; www.texashotelvegas.com), or step into the dark confines of the **Liberty Bar** (1618 E 6th Ave; www.thelibertyaustin.com) if you want to hide out while sipping your well-crafted Texas Mule.

❸ White Horse

Well, of course there's a honky-tonk next to a glossy apartment complex. And since this is Austin, it just seems to work. An easy-going bar and mini dance hall just off 6th St, **White Horse** (p62) is a good place to learn to two-step – it offers lessons before the band starts. There are craft beers aplenty plus whiskey on tap. Patio and food truck too.

❹ Craft Cocktails

Sexy lighting and top-notch libations keep everyone happy – and looking fine – at busy and high-ceilinged **Whisler's** (p62).

❺ Cheap & Loud

No, we're not talking about your ex. We're talking about the **Violet Crown Social Club** (p63). With crafts beers, an intimate and dark interior, a dog-friendly patio and an awesome food truck (of course) serving up hearty Detroit-style pizza from **Via 313** (www.via313.com), this is a darn fun place to end the evening.

East Austin

MUELLER

MLK

HANCOCK

CHERRYWOOD

EAST AUSTIN

Tilley St

Manor Rd

Sorin St

E. M. Franklin Ave

Pershing Dr

E Martin Luther King Jr Blvd

E 12th St

Berkman Dr

Tom Miller St

Southwest Greenway

Anchor La

Antone St

Tillery St

E 18th St

E 17th St

E 16th St

Harvey St

E 13th St

Thinkery
3

Mueller Lake Park

Zach Scott St

Cornacho St

Manor Rd

Airport Blvd

21

Airport Blvd

Evergreen Cemetery

Northwest Greenway

Airport Blvd

Patterson Neighborhood Park

Schieffer Ave

E 40th St

Willowbrook Reach

Clifford Ave

Alexander Ave

Downs-Mabson Fields

E 14th St

Wiltshire Blvd

Cherrywood Rd

E 22nd St

Cedar Ave

Martin Luther King Jr

E 17th St

E 14th St

E 41st St

E 38th 1/2 St

Concordia Ave

Edgewood Ave

E 32nd St

Maple Ave

14

Singleton Ave

Chestnut Ave

35

290

Interregional Hwy

E 30th St

E 28th St

Coledo St

Alamo St

Poquito St

8 9

13

Chicon St

Leona St

Red River St

Mount Calvary Cemetery

Manor Rd

E 22nd St

E 21st St

E 20th St

Comal St

E Martin Luther King Jr Blvd

Comal St

Oakwood Cemetery

Eastwoods Neighbourhood Park

E Dean Keeton St

University of Texas at Austin

Red River St

E Martin Luther King Jr Blvd

E 15th St

1 km

0.5 miles

For reviews see

⊙ Sights	p56
⊗ Eating	p58
◖◗ Drinking	p62
✦ Entertainment	p63

East Austin

Airport Blvd

Austin
Bouldering
Project
● 1

⊗ 15

E 7th St

E 5th St

E Cesar Chavez St (E 1st St)

Red Bluff Rd

Colorado River

The Basin

Kirk Ave

Mansell Ave

Shady La

Springdale Rd

Gunter St

19 ⊖

Cherico St

Gonzales St

Gunter St

Oak Springs Dr

Goodwin Ave

Tillery St

Govalle Ave

Neal Ave

Stokes Dr

Lyons Rd

Castro St

Prado St

Garwood St

Tillery St

Linden St

GOVALLE

Boggy Creek

N Pleasant Valley Rd

Zaragosa
Park

Hidalgo St

E 5th St

N Pleasant Valley Rd

Thompson St

Hargrave St

Neal St

Nile St

Boggy Creek
Greenbelt

Northwestern Ave

Weber/Miller

E 10th St

E 8th St

E 7th St

Poquito St

Lincoln St

E 6th St

Santa Maria St

San Saba St

Canterbury St

HOLLY

Pedernales St

Mildred St

Metz
Park

**EAST
AUSTIN**

New York Ave

Pennsylvania Ave

S L Davis Ave

Rosewood Ave

George Washington
Carver Museum
2 ⊘

Salina St

Chicon St

Comal St

Concho St

E 11th St

Texas State
Cemetery

16 ⊘

17 ⊖

4 ●

E 5th St

E 4th St

E 3rd St

Chicon St

6 ⊘

Willow St

Robert Martinez Jr St

Anthony St

12 ⊘

Lynn St

Haskell St

Canterbury St

Riverview St

Martin
Middle
School

HOLLY

E 14th St

E 13th St

E 12th St

Comal St

Navasota St

Olive St

Curve St

Branch St

⊗ 10

E 11th St

E 10th St

E 9th St

Lydia St

⊗ 11

Navasota St

⊘ 18

Waller St

E 7th St

E 6th St

San Marcos St

Plaza M ⊖ 17
Saltillo

E 3rd St

E 2nd St

E Cesar Chavez St (E 1st St)

Garden St

Willow St

Holly St

⊘ 7

20 ⊘

6 ⊘

**EAST
CESAR
CHAVEZ**

Ladybird Lake

Interregional Hwy

Interregional Hwy

Red River St

E 14th St

Juniper St

E 11th St

E 10th St

E 8th St

Red River St

P

East Ave

290

Sights

Austin Bouldering Project

CLIMBING

1 ⊙ MAP P54, F6

If a fear of ropes and harnesses has kept you from rock climbing, give bouldering a try here. The climbing heights are typically 13ft to 15ft, with a few stretching higher. A thick floor pad will cushion your fall. Bright and airy, the complex has a 2nd-floor viewing area, and the place has a positive and communal vibe. (☎512-645-4633; www.austinboulderingproject.com; 979 Springdale Rd; day pass adult/child $16/12, shoe rental $4; ☉6am-11pm Mon-Fri, 9am-10pm Sat & Sun)

George Washington Carver Museum

MUSEUM

2 ⊙ MAP P54, B5

On June 19, 1865, slaves in Texas were freed pursuant to the Emancipation Proclamation, two and a half years after it was signed by President Lincoln. This day is now honored as Juneteenth, and an exhibit at this small museum examines its history. The museum also holds a few personal items of African American botanist and inventor George Washington Carver. (www.austintexas.gov; 1165 Angelina St; admission free; ☉10am-6pm Mon-Wed, to 9pm Thu, to 5pm Fri, to 4pm Sat; ♿)

Thinkery

MUSEUM

3 ⊙ MAP P54, E1

This huge, red, box-like building north of downtown inspires young minds with hands-on activities in the realms of science, technology and the arts. Kids can get wet learning about fluid dynamics, build LED light structures and explore chemical reactions in the Kitchen Lab, among other attractions. A spectacular outdoor play area holds nets and climbing toys. Closed Monday except for Baby Bloomers and other special events. (☎512-469-6200; www.thinkeryaustin.org; 1830 Simond Ave; adult/child under 2yr $12/free; ☉10am-5pm Tue, Thu & Fri, to 8pm Wed, to 6pm Sat & Sun; ♿)

Texas State Cemetery

CEMETERY

4 ⊙ MAP P54, B6

Revitalized in the 1990s, the state's official cemetery is the final resting place of key figures from Texan history. Interred here are luminaries including Stephen F Austin, Miriam 'Ma' Ferguson (the state's first female governor), writer James Michener and Lone Star State flag designer Joanna Troutman, along with thousands of soldiers who died in the Civil War, plus more than 100 leaders of the Republic of Texas who were exhumed from other sites and reburied here. Self-guided-tour brochures are usually available from the visitor center. The cemetery is just north of E 7th St. (☎512-463-0605; 909 Navasota St; ☉8am-5pm daily, visitor center 8am-5pm Mon-Fri)

Thinkery

Eating

Franklin Barbecue

BARBECUE $

5 ✖ MAP P54, B5

This famous BBQ joint only serves lunch, and only until it runs out – usually well before 2pm. To avoid missing out, join the line – and there will be a line – by 10am (9am on weekends). Treat it as a tailgating party: bring beer or mimosas to share and make friends. And yes, you do want the fatty brisket. (📞512-653-1187; www.franklinbbq. com; 900 E 11th St; sandwiches $7-12.50, ribs/brisket per lb $19/25; 🕑11am-2pm Tue-Sun)

Tacos

BRANDON ROSENBLUM/GETTY IMAGES ©

Veracruz All Natural

MEXICAN $

6 ✖ MAP P54, B7

Two sisters from Mexico run this East Austin taco truck (an old bus), which may serve the best tacos in town. Step up to the window, order a *migas* breakfast taco (you must!) then add a quesadilla or torta for variety. Take your buzzer – yep, this food truck has a buzzer – and grab a picnic table. (📞512-981-1760; www.veracruzallnatural.com; 1704 E Cesar Chavez St; tacos $3-4, mains $8; 🕑7am-3pm)

Cenote

CAFE $

7 ✖ MAP P54, A7

One of our favorite cafes in Austin, Cenote uses seasonal, largely organic ingredients in its simple but delicious anytime fare. Come for housemade granola and yogurt with fruit, banh mi sandwiches and couscous curry. The cleverly shaded patio is a fine retreat for a rich coffee or a craft beer (or perhaps a handmade popsicle from Juju). (1010 E Cesar Chavez St; mains $8-15; 🕑7am-10pm Mon-Fri, from 8am Sat, 8am-4pm Sun; 🛜)

Mi Madre's

MEXICAN $

8 ✖ MAP P54, C3

Barbacoa, chorizo and *adobado* are just a few of the authentic Mexican specialties here. In fact, it was recommended by a friend who said the *barbacoa* was just like his grandma used to make. Praise

BBQ in Lockhart

The city of Lockhart may be 30 miles southeast of Austin, but when you're talking about a place that's home to four outstanding BBQ restaurants, a short drive is not an issue. How good is Lockhart? Well, in 1999, the Texas Legislature adopted a resolution naming Lockhart the barbecue capital of Texas. Of course, that means it's the barbecue capital of the world. You can eat very well for under $15.

Black's Barbecue (512-398-2712; www.blacksbbq.com; 215 N Main St; sandwiches $7-12, brisket per lb $20; 10am-8pm Sun-Thu, to 8:30pm Fri & Sat) A longtime Lockhart favorite since 1932, with sausage so good Lyndon Johnson had them cater a party at the nation's capital.

Kreuz Market (512-398-2361; www.kreuzmarket.com; 619 N Colorado St; brisket per lb $18.50; 10:30am-8pm Mon-Sat, to 6pm Sun) Serving Lockhart since 1900, the barnlike Kreuz Market uses a dry rub, which means you shouldn't insult them by asking for barbecue sauce; they don't serve it, and the meat doesn't need it.

Chisholm Trail Bar-B-Q (512-398-6027; www.lockhartchisholm trailbbq.com; 1323 S Colorado St; lunch plates $7.50-15, brisket per lb $14; 7am-8pm Mon-Wed, to 9pm Thu-Sat, 8am-8pm Sun) Like Black's and Kreuz, Chisholm Trail has been named one of the top 10 barbecue restaurants in the state by *Texas Monthly* magazine. Has a drive-through if you're in a hurry.

Smitty's Market (512-398-9344; www.smittysmarket.com; 208 S Commerce St; brisket per lb $14.90; 7am-6pm Mon-Fri, to 6:30pm Sat, 9am-6:30pm Sun) The blackened pit room and homely dining room are all original (knives used to be chained to the tables). Ask them to trim off the fat on the brisket if you're particular about that.

doesn't come much higher than that. Before dinner, enjoy a drink at the mezcal bar on the roof. (512-322-9721; www.mimadresrestaurant.com; 2201 Manor Rd; tacos $3-5, mains $9-14; 6am-2pm Mon & Tue, to 10pm Wed-Sat, 8am-4pm Sun)

El Chilito

TEX-MEX $

9 MAP P54, C3

If you want quick, cheap and easy, this walk-up taco stand (with a big deck for your dining pleasure) can't be beat. You've got to try breakfast tacos while you're in Austin, and this is a good place

UNIVERSITY OF COLLEGE/SHUTTERSTOCK ©

Black's Barbecue (p59), Lockhart

to get them. (📞512-382-3797; www.
elchilito.com; 2219 Manor Rd; tacos &
burritos $3-9; ⏱7am-10pm Mon-Fri,
from 8am Sat & Sun)

Paperboy   AMERICAN, BREAKFAST $

10 MAP P54, B6

Even the food trucks here are
going hyper local, 'curating'
menus based on what's available.
Breakfast wunderkind Paperboy
does this particularly well, luring
in-the-know locals with gourmet
breakfast sandwiches. A recent
menu featured an egg-covered
pimiento cheese and bacon sandwich and a sweet-potato hash with
braised pork belly and kale. (www.
paperboyaustin.com; 1203 E 11th St;
mains $7-9; ⏱7am-2pm Tue-Fri, 8am-
2pm Sat & Sun)

Licha's Cantina   MEXICAN $$

11 MAP P54, B6

This cozy cottage may lure you in
with its $5 drink specials at happy
hour (4pm to 6pm Tuesday to
Friday), but the interior Mexican
dishes will have you sticking
around. Eat inside, or in the yard
out front, or settle in at the bar
where the conversations are intriguing and the service top-notch.
(www.lichascantina.com; 1306 E 6th
St; mains $13-27; ⏱4-11pm Tue-Thu,
4pm-midnight Fri, noon-midnight Sat,
11am-3pm Sun)

Launderette   MODERN AMERICAN $$

12 MAP P54, C8

A brilliant repurposing of a former
washeteria, Launderette has a
stylish, streamlined design that

provides a fine backdrop to the delicious Mediterranean-inspired cooking. Among the many hits: crab toast, wood-grilled octopus, Brussels sprouts with apple-bacon marmalade, a perfectly rendered brick chicken and whole grilled branzino. (📞512-382-1599; www.launderetteaustin.com; 2115 Holly St; mains $18-42; ⏰11am-2:30pm daily, 5-10pm Sun-Thu, to 11pm Fri & Sat)

Salty Sow
AMERICAN $$

13 ✖ MAP P54, C3

Behold the porcine wonder! This snout-to-tail restaurant advertising 'swine + wine' offers a thoroughly modern take on down-home cooking, including plenty of choices in the nonpork category. (📞512-391-2337; www.saltysow.com; 1917 Manor Rd; small plates $8-12, mains $16-24; ⏰4:30-10pm Sun-Thu, to 11pm Fri & Sat)

Dai Due
AMERICAN $$$

14 ✖ MAP P54, C3

Even an eggs-and-sausage breakfast is a meal to remember at this lauded East Austin favorite. All ingredients come from Texas farms, rivers and hunting grounds, as well as the Gulf of Mexico. Supper Club dinners spotlight items like wild game and foraged treats. Like your cut of meat? See if the attached butcher shop has a few pounds to go. (📞512-719-3332; www.daidue.com; 2406 Manor Rd; breakfast & lunch $13-22, dinner $21-69; ⏰11am-3pm & 5-10pm Tue-Fri, from 10am Sat & Sun)

Justine's
FRENCH $$$

15 ✖ MAP P54, E8

With a lovely garden setting festooned with fairy lights, Justine's is a top spot for wowing a date. French onion soup, seared scallops and grilled pork chop are standouts on the small, classic brasserie

---

Heading out in East Austin

Bar-hopping on E 6th St The block east of I-35 turns vibrant as the sun goes down and the dive bars and eateries fill with hip and festive crowds.

Farm-to-table fare Austin foodies rave about the carefully crafted dishes that embrace regional bounty, from wild game at Dai Due (p62) to the pork at Salty Sow, to the locally sourced breakfast at Paperboy food truck.

Neighborhood dining and drinking Insiders have long loved the traditional Mexican dishes at Mi Madre's (p58), but now they keep the party going at the mescal bar upstairs.

Bar on 6th St

menu. There are also a few more creative changing daily specials like pan-seared quail with parsnip casserole or grilled swordfish with artichokes and cauliflower puree. (📞512-385-2900; www.justines1937. com; 4710 E 5th St; mains $20-28; ⏱6pm-2am Wed-Mon)

Drinking

Whisler's   COCKTAIL BAR

16 📍 MAP P54, B6

If vampires walk the streets of East Austin, then this dark and moody cocktail bar is surely where they congregate before a night of feeding. And we don't quite trust that taxidermied boar overlooking the bar from his lofty perch. Head to the patio for a less intimate scene, as well as live music. (📞512-480-0781; www.whislersatx.com; 1816 E 6th St; ⏱4pm-2am)

White Horse   LIVE MUSIC

17 📍 MAP P54, B6

Ladies, you will be asked to dance at this East Austin honky-tonk, where two-steppers and hipsters mingle like siblings in a diverse but happy family. Play pool, take a dance lesson or step outside to sip a microbrew on the patio. Live music nightly – only on weekends is a (small) cover charged – and whiskey on tap. We like this place. (www.thewhitehorseaustin.com; 500 Comal St; ⏱3pm-2am)

Violet Crown Social Club

BAR

18 🚇 MAP P54, B6

It's dark. It's loud. At first glance it's not terribly inviting. But damn, the drinks are cheap, making this a popular spot on the East 6th circuit. (1111 E 6th St; ⏰5pm-2am)

Sa-Ten Coffee & Eats

COFFEE

19 🚇 MAP P54, E7

If you're on the east side of town and need a caffeine jolt, head to this bright and minimalist box for top-notch coffees and a small menu of Japanese snacks. This busy place is tucked among galleries and studios in the Canopy Austin artist complex. There are outside tables if you need some sunshine. (📞512-524-1544; www.sa-ten.com; 916 Springdale Rd; ⏰7am-10pm; 📶)

Flat Track Coffee

COFFEE

20 🚇 MAP P54, B7

This East Austin java joint also houses a bicycle repair shop. Or maybe it's the other way around. Either way, this former coffee-catering company is the go-to spot for coffee aficionados east of the I-35. On weekends, you'll find a food truck out front selling mini-donuts. Cycles also for rent. (📞512-814-6010; www.flattrackcoffee.com; 1619 E Cesar Chavez St; ⏰7am-7pm)

Entertainment

Skylark Lounge

BLUES

21 ⭐ MAP P54, E3

It's a bit of a drive (2.5 miles northeast of downtown), but well worth the effort to reach this friendly dive bar that serves up live blues – along with fairly priced drinks, free popcorn and a shaded patio. (📞512-730-0759; www.skylarkaustin.com; 2039 Airport Blvd; ⏰5pm-midnight Mon-Fri, to 1am Sat, to 10pm Sun)

East Austin Entertainment

Explore ◈

South Austin

This quirky but festive neighborhood – especially along S Congress Ave – is the city's soul. Tourism types nicknamed it SoCo, which has somewhat stuck, but locals mostly call it South Congress. The road is the main thoroughfare through the neighborhood and the epicenter of the action; most of the rest is residential, although burgeoning S 1st St has been been seeing more commercial activity in recent years.

The Short List

○ **Broken Spoke (p83)** *Joining a two-stepping lesson on a Saturday night.*

○ **Bat Colony (p67)** *Taking in a lake tour with Capital Cruises to watch the evening migration of the bats.*

○ **Continental Club (p83)** *Listening to Dale Watson sing his country and western songs.*

○ **Amy's Ice Creams (p78)** *Gobbling down artisan ice cream in the thick of the South Congress parade.*

○ **Barton Springs Pool (p69)** *Hopping in the spring-fed water to cool off on a hot Texas afternoon.*

○ **Ann & Roy Butler Hike-and-Bike Trail & Boardwalk (p76)** *Checking out the downtown skyline from the lakeside boardwalk.*

Getting There & Around

🚗 From downtown, follow Congress Ave south over Lady Bird Lake.

🚲 There are three B-cycle stations on S Congress Ave.

🚌 Bus 1 connects S Congress Ave with downtown then travels along Lavaca St to Guadalupe St near UT to N Lamar Blvd.

South Austin Map on p74

View over Barton Creek Greenbelt (p76) TRONG NGUYEN/GETTY IMAGES ©

Top Experience 📷

Watch the Nightly Bat Swarm Under Congress Avenue Bridge

Looking very much like a special effect from a B movie, a funnel cloud of up to 1.5 million Mexican free-tailed bats swarms from under the Congress Avenue Bridge nightly from late March to early November. Turns out Austin isn't just the live-music capital of the world; it's also home to the largest urban bat population in North America.

👁 MAP P74, G2

Congress Ave

🕐 sunset Apr-Nov

Bat Story

The Congress Avenue Bridge was built in 1910. After improvements to the bridge in 1980, a colony of Mexican free-tailed bats moved in. Apparently the bats like the bridge's nooks and crannies for roosting. These tiny winged mammals live in Mexico in the winter then migrate north when Austin warms up. They typically swarm out at twilight to feed. The colony is made up entirely of female and young animals. Such is the bat-density that bat-radars have detected bat-columns up to 10,000ft (3050m) high. In June, each female gives birth to one pup, and every night at dusk, the families take to the skies in search of food.

Bat Viewing from Land

It's become an Austin tradition to head to Lady Bird Lake to watch the bats swarm out to feed on an estimated 10,000lb to 20,000lb of insects per night. The swarm looks a lot like a fast-moving, black, chittering river. Best places on land for viewing? One easy spot is the sidewalk on the eastern side of the bridge. You can also try the grassy lawn behind the Austin-American Statesman building at 305 S Congress Ave, on the southeast end of the bridge. Parking in the Statesman lot is $6 for four hours. Don't miss this nightly show. The best viewing is in August.

Bat Cruises & Kayak Tours

To add a little adventure to your bat watching, view the bats from a boat or kayak on Lady Bird Lake. During bat season, **Lone Star Riverboat** (☎512-327-1388; www.lonestarriverboat.com; adult/child $10/7; ☉Mar–mid-Dec) offers nightly sunset bat-watching trips on its 32ft electric cruiser. The company's dock is on the south shore of Lady Bird Lake near the Hyatt; **Capital Cruises** (☎512-480-9264; www.capitalcruises.com; adult/child $10/5) also runs tours. **Live Love Paddle** (www.livelovepaddle.com) and **Congress Avenue Kayaks** (www.congresskayaks.com) offer guided evening bat tours.

★ Top Tips

◦ To find out what time the bats will probably emerge during your visit, call the **Bat Hotline** at 512-327-9721 ext 3.

✕ Take a Break

Many good restaurants line S Congress Ave south of the bridge. For Tex-Mex and a lively scene, head to Güero's Taco Bar (p81).

For ice cream, try Amy's Ice Creams (p78) where they'll mix – or smash – your choice of toppings into your scoops.

Top Experience

Enjoy the Outdoors at Zilker Park

Established through a series of gifts by local businessman Andrew Jackson Zilker, this 350-acre park is a slice of green heaven, lined with hiking and biking trails. It celebrated its 100th birthday in 2017. The park also provides access to the famed Barton Springs natural swimming pool and Barton Creek Greenbelt. Other attractions include a botanical garden, kayak rentals, a nature center, disc golf and a miniature train.

◉ **MAP P74, B1**

☏ 512-974-6700

www.austintexas.gov/
department/zilker-metro-
politan-park

2100 Barton Springs Rd

🕐 5am-10pm

Barton Springs Pool

Hot? Not for long. Even when the temperature hits 100, you'll be shivering in a jiff after you jump into this icy-cold natural-spring **pool** (adult/child $9/5; ⏱5am-10pm). The pool is fed by the Edwards Aquifer, which flows to the springs through limestone channels. The Moderne-style bathhouse was built in 1947. Draped with century-old pecan trees, the area around the pool is a social scene in itself, and the place gets packed on hot summer days. You'll even see folks swimming laps – with a lifeguard on duty – in February!

Zilker Botanical Garden

These lush **gardens** (☎512-477-8672; www.zilkergarden.org; 2220 Barton Springs Rd; adult/child $3/1; ⏱9am-5pm, to 7pm during daylight saving time) cover 31 acres on the south bank of Lady Bird Lake, with displays including natural grottoes, a Japanese garden and a fragrant herb garden. You'll also find interesting historical artifacts sprinkled about, including a 19th-century pioneer cabin, a cupola that once sat atop a local schoolhouse, and a footbridge moved from Congress Ave.

Umlauf Sculpture Garden

If the weather's too perfect to be indoors, stroll the open-air **Umlauf Sculpture Garden** (☎512-445-5582; www.umlaufsculpture.org; 605 Robert E Lee Rd; adult/child under 12yr/student $5/free/1; ⏱10am-4pm Tue-Fri, noon-4pm Sat & Sun) at the southern end of the park. Within the garden and the indoor museum there are more than 130 works by 20th-century sculptor Charles Umlauf, who was an art professor at UT for 40 years.

Austin Nature & Science Center

In the northwestern area of the park, this **center** (☎512-974-3888; www.austintexas.gov/department/austin-nature-science-center; 301 Nature Center Dr; donations requested; ⏱9am-5pm Mon-Sat, noon-5pm Sun) has exhibitions of native Texan mammals, birds, reptiles, amphibians and arthropods that have been injured and nursed back to health here but cannot be released back into the wild.

★ **Top Tips**

o To get out on the lake, rent a kayak or canoe with **Zilker Park Boat Rentals** (☎512-478-3852; www.zilkerboats.com; 2101 Andrew Zilker Rd; per hour/day $15/45; ⏱10am-dusk). To find the rental facility, turn left immediately after entering the park from Barton Springs Rd. The canoes are below the parking lot, on the shore of the creek. Look for the 'Canoe Rental is Open' banner.

o On weekends from April to early September, admission is $5 per car. The $3 admission fee for Zilker Botanical Garden is cash or check only.

✕ **Take a Break**

After wandering the sculpture or botanical gardens, drive to Elizabeth Street Cafe (p81) for a light French-Vietnamese lunch or a pastry.

Top Experience 📷

Discover the Flora of Texas at Lady Bird Johnson Wildflower Center

Anyone with an interest in Texas' flora and fauna should make the 20-minute drive to the Lady Bird Johnson Wildflower Center, southwest of downtown Austin. The center, founded with the assistance of Texas' beloved former First Lady, features every type of wildflower and plant that grows in Texas, separated by geographical region, with an emphasis on Hill Country flora.

◎ MAP P74, A5

📞 512-232-0100

www.wildflower.org

4801 La Crosse Ave

adult/child 5-17yr/student & senior $10/4/8

🕘 9am-5pm Tue-Sun

Lady Bird Johnson

Lady Bird Johnson's belief that beautiful surroundings could boost the morale and mental health of Americans was the driving force behind her national beautification efforts during her husband Lyndon B Johnson's presidency. One straightforward solution she supported? Cleaning up neglected medians and highway right-of-ways with green landscaping and wildflowers. She had tremendous success with this vision in Texas, and today highway right-of-ways are groomed and seeded with wildflowers by the Texas Department of Transportation. She created the National Wildflower Research Center in 1982 with actress Helen Hayes. It outgrew its original East Austin home, moving south of the city to its current location in 1995, and was renamed in her honor two years later.

Central Gardens

These sustainable gardens showcase many of the 650 species of native plants found across the 284-acre center. Sustainable plants help to sustain the environment through various methods that conserve water, support wildlife and otherwise help the surrounding ecosystem. The dry creek bed garden, for example, absorbs and filters the pollutants in rain water through the use of low depressions near polluting run-off sources. The pollinator habitat garden is an open-air garden created to attract and support butterflies and other pollinators.

Family Garden

This is a pretty place to let youngsters explore, learn and blow off steam, with the added bonus of a gorgeous backdrop for parents to enjoy. Immersive features in this 4.5-acre garden include a shrub maze, a lazy creek, a tree 'stumpery' with giant stumps, and a grotto with caves and a waterfall. Great for a photo are the over-sized bird nests made from grape vines. Even the adults will want to step inside to experience what it might feel like to be a baby bird.

★ Top Tips

○ Spring is the best time to visit, but there's something in bloom all year.

○ Check the website before your visit to see what flowers are in season.

○ Stretch your legs on 2 miles of trails.

○ The Wildflower Center hosts a variety of events during National Wildflower Week in May.

✗ Take a Break

On-site, the **Wildflower Cafe** serves salads, sandwiches and hibiscus mint iced tea. A few kids' options are available too.

For a drink in an aesthetically pleasing spot in South Austin, take a seat on the patio at the Hotel San José (p82).

Walking Tour 🚶

South Congress Stroll

You won't find any chain stores along S Congress Ave, and the indie shops here are truly unique. Which explains the heavy flow of pedestrians filling those sidewalks on weekends and on weekday evenings. Cafes, coffee shops and dessert spots are also temptingly easy to find. People-watching is superb.

Walk Facts

Start Lucy in Disguise
End Tesoros Trading Co
Length 0.5 miles; 15 minutes

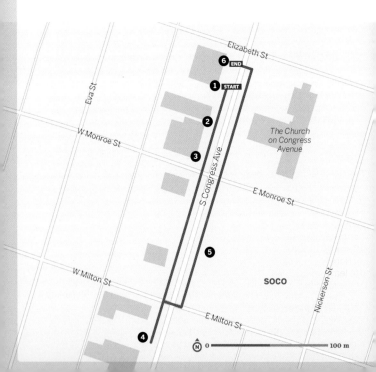

❶ Costume Central

If you want to get a jump on your costume shopping for Halloween, **Lucy in Disguise** (p85) is the place to go. Outfits and costumes are arranged by genre, from burlesque to Ancient Rome, and by decade, including the '70s, baby. It's a fun place to start a stroll, with costumes and occasionally wacky vintage duds highlighting the joyful weirdness of Austin.

❷ Antiques Here, There & Everywhere

Take a breath. You're going to be spending some time in **Uncommon Objects** (512-442-4000; 1512 S Congress Ave; 11am-7pm Sun-Thu, to 8pm Fri & Sat), an enticing antique mall where more than 20 vendors show off a packed-tight array of antiques. Many of these finds would look right at home in your rustic chic digs back home.

❸ Boots Galore

Be careful in here. Looking at the towering aisles of men's and women's cowboy boots – all arranged by shoe size – at **Allens Boots** (512-447-1413; www.allensboots. com; 1522 S Congress Ave; 9am-8pm Mon-Sat, noon-6pm Sun) is akin to looking at puppies. It's hard to leave empty-handed; you *are* in Texas after all. Makers include Lucchese, Justin, Tony Lama and Frye. Hats and accessories sold here too.

❹ Candy, Candy, Candy

Willy Wonka would be impressed by **Big Top Candy Shop** (512-462-2220; www.bigtopcandyshop.com; 1706 S Congress Ave; 11am-7pm Sun-Thu, 11am-9pm Fri, 10am-9pm Sat;), a narrow store that manages to cram in an amazing array of sweet delights, from classics to modern favorites. The array of gummy treats is astounding. Also sells ice cream. For bulk purchases, head to the bins and scoops in back.

❺ Style & Hospitality

Walk across S Congress Ave to check out the sleek **South Congress Hotel** (p82). And while the decor is minimalist cool, we swear this place has the nicest valets around. Inside, the gift shop has a few unique finds and you'll see a couple of good patios for snacking and people-watching. Or grab an iced coffee at Café No Sé. Motorcycle enthusiasts dig the bikes at Revival Cycles (www.revivalcycles. com), where the handcrafted rides could double as works of art. Make that *badass* art, of course.

❻ Treat Yourself at Tesoros

Continue back up S Congress Ave, crossing over to **Tesoros Trading Co** (512-447-7500; 1500 S Congress Ave; 11am-6pm Sun-Fri, 10am-6pm Sat). Well-stocked with colorful and unique arts-and-crafts, many with a Latin influence, it's a good spot for an end-of-stroll personal reward.

A **B** **C** **D**

0 500 m
0 0,25 miles

12

1

Zilker Park

Barton Springs Rd

Barton Creek

2 Barton Creek Greenbelt

Barton Creek

Barton Creek

Barton Springs

2

BARTON HILLS

Barton Hills Dr

Robert E Lee Rd

Lund St

Barton Blvd

Virginia Ave

Lindscomb Ave

Kerr St

Garrider Ave

Kinney Ave

Treadwell St

Juliet St

For reviews see

◉ Top Experiences p66
◉ Sights p76
✖ Eating p78
🍷 Drinking p82
★ Entertainment p83
🔒 Shopping p84

Bluebonnet La

Folts Ave

Dexter St

Treadwell St

Margaret St

Dexter St

3

Ashby Ave

Oxford Ave

Dwyer Ave

Lamar Square Dr

25

11

Rundell Pl

Anita Dr

ZILKER

Collier St

27

Paramount Ave

Ann Arbor Ave

Bluebonnet La

Ford St

Nash Ave

Bauerle Ave

Kinney Ave

SouthPop

6

4

Rabb Rd

De Verne St

Rabb Glen St

Goodrich Ave

Hether St

Oxford Ave

S Lamar Blvd

S 7th St

Arpdale St

29

33

S 6th St

S 5th St

Ricky Guerrero Park

W Live Oak St

La Casa Dr

S Lamar Blvd

5

8

23

Del Curto Rd

SOUTH LAMAR

Thornton Rd

20

W Oltorf St

Southwood Rd

Fieldcrest Dr

S 5th St

Lady Bird Johnson Wildflower Center

(9mi)

6

South Austin Neighborhood Park

Herndon La

Lightsey Rd

7

A **B** **C** **D**

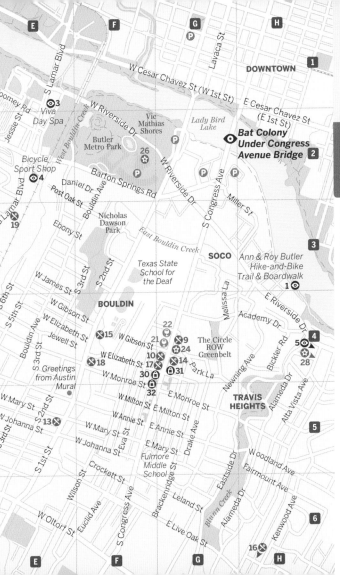

Sights

Ann & Roy Butler Hike-and-Bike Trail & Boardwalk

VIEWPOINT

1 ◉ MAP P74, H3

You can gaze at the downtown skyline from a series of photogenic boardwalks on this scenic 10-mile trail, which loops around Lady Bird Lake. Shorten the loop by crossing the lake on one of several bridges. You'll find restrooms, water fountains and waste bags for your pet along the way. Check the city's Parks & Recreation webpage for parking lots, trail access points and ADA accessible entrances.

Austin old-timers may refer to the trail as the Lady Bird Trail or the Town Lake Trail. (www.austintexas. gov/department/parks-and-recreation; 1820 Lakeshore Blvd; ⏰5am-midnight; 👫 😺)

Barton Creek Greenbelt

PARK

2 ◉ MAP P74, B1

From Zilker Park, this refreshing multiuse path unfurls for more than 8 miles along Barton Creek. Hike (p86), bike and splash around. There are several access points, including the entry path near 1601 Spyglass Rd. Leashed dogs OK. (www.austintexas.gov; 3753 S Capital of Texas Hwy)

Murals of South Austin

Most people know about Austin's awesome food trucks, but the city is also home to an amazing collection of murals and wall art. Quirky, funny and sometimes poignant, the murals are unexpected treasures that bring a little joy to routine drives around the city. A few memorable images cluster in South Austin along S 1st St and Congress Ave. Two good choices for snap-happy visitors:

Greetings from Austin (Map p74, E5; 1720 S 1st St) This bright mural on W Annie St doubles as an Instagram postcard. While you're here, someone will probably walk up to take a photo because it's awesome. The eye-catching mural adorns the southside of the Roadhouse Relics building.

I Love You So Much (1300 S Congress Ave) There could well be a line waiting to take a selfie in front of this simple expression of devotion, spray-painted on the side of Jo's Coffee (p82) in South Congress. It now joins the Austin Motel sign and the patio at Güero's (p81) as an iconic symbol of the neighborhood. It was a declaration of affection, we hear, for a local hotelier from her girlfriend. Eagle-eyed visitors may spot funny spin-offs of the mural around town.

Viva Day Spa   SPA

3 ◉ MAP P74, E1

Repeatedly named 'Best Spa' in the *Austin Chronicle's* Best of Austin awards, Viva is conveniently located downtown so you can steal a few moments of pampering during your visit. (☎512-300-2256; www.vivadayspa.com; 215 S Lamar Blvd; ⊙9am-8pm)

Bicycle Sport Shop   CYCLING

4 ◉ MAP P74, E2

The great thing about Bicycle Sport Shop is its proximity to Zilker Park, Barton Springs and the Lady Bird Lake bike paths, all of which are within a few blocks. Rentals range from $16 for a two-hour cruise on a standard bike, to $62 for a full day on a top-end full-suspension model. On weekends and holidays, advance reservations are advised. (☎512-477-3472; www.bicyclesportshop.com; 517 S Lamar Blvd; per 2hr from $16; ⊙10am-7pm Mon-Fri, 9am-6pm Sat, 11am-5pm Sun)

Roy G Guerrero Disc Golf Course   GOLF

5 ◉ MAP P74, H4

A disc-golf course with 18 holes suitable for beginners and skilled players alike. (517 S Pleasant Valley Rd; admission free; ⊙sunrise–sunset)

Ann & Roy Butler Hike-and-Bike Trail & Boardwalk

TRONG NGUYEN/SHUTTERSTOCK ©

South Austin Sights

SouthPop   CULTURAL CENTER

6 ◉ MAP P74, D4

Pop into this South Austin gallery for rotating exhibits that spotlight Austin's live music and entertainment scenes, from the 1960s to the present. (South Austin Popular Cultural Center; ☎512-440-8318; www.southpop.org; 1516-B S Lamar Ave; admission free; ⊙1-6pm Thu-Sun)

Cathedral of Junk   SCULPTURE

7 ◉ MAP P74, D6

An ongoing (and climbable!) backyard sculpture that turns one man's trash into everyone's treasure. Visitation is by

Lady Bird Lake: What's Your Name, Again?

What's the name of the body of water dividing downtown from South Austin? Well, it might depend on who you're asking. The lake is a reservoir along the Colorado River, formed after the completion of Longhorn Dam in 1960. For decades the lake was known simply as Town Lake. This changed in 2007 after the Austin city council renamed it Lady Bird Lake in honor of the former First Lady, who was behind lakeside beautification efforts. The trail around the park was then dubbed Lady Bird Lake Trail. That name was changed to the Ann & Roy Butler Hike-and-Bike Trail in 2011 to honor former mayor Roy Butler and his wife Ann. To add to the confusion, the Colorado River reservoir below Mount Bonnell northwest of downtown is known as Lake Austin. Got it? No worries if you don't – you'll hear all of these various names, and no one will fuss with you if you get it wrong.

appointment, by phone. Owner Vince Hanneman doesn't always get to his voicemail, so keep trying until he answers. He'll fill you in on parking. Note that you can't really see the cathedral from a drive-by. (☎512-299-7413; 4422 Lareina Dr; requested donation per group $10; ☉by appointment)

Veloway Track   CYCLING

8 MAP P74, A5

Plan some extra time to ride or skate the great 3.1-mile Veloway track, near the Lady Bird Johnson Wildflower Center. The track runs clockwise, and no walking or running is permitted. (www.veloway. com; 4900 La Crosse Ave; admission free; ☉dawn-dusk)

Eating

Amy's Ice Creams – South Austin   ICE CREAM $

9 ✖ MAP P74, G4

The South Congress location of this beloved local ice-cream chain shares its daily flavors on a chalkboard out front. Pick your favorite add-on, and they'll pound it into your ice-cream choice. (☎512-440-7488; www.amysicecreams.com; 1301 S Congress; ice cream $3.25-6; ☉11:30am-11pm Sun-Thu, to midnight Fri & Sat)

Hopdoddy Burger Bar   BURGERS $

10 ✖ MAP P74, G4

Folks line up around the block for burgers, fries and shakes – and it's not because they're hard to come by in Austin. It's because the Hopdoddy chain's flagship outlet slathers love into everything it makes, from the humanely raised beef to the locally sourced ingredients to the fresh-baked buns. The sleek, modern building is pretty sweet, too. (☎ 512-243-7505; www.hopdoddy.com; 1400 S Congress Ave; burgers $7-13; ◷ 5pm-3am Sun-Thu, to 4am Fri & Sat; 🛜)

Ramen Tatsu-ya RAMEN $

11 ❌ MAP P74, D3

With its communal tables, loud indie music and hustling efficiency, we wouldn't say this busy ramen joint is a relaxing experience, but darn, is it good. Step up to the counter – there will be a line – and take your pick of seven noodle-and-veggie-loaded broths. Like it spicy? Order the Mi-So-Hot. You can also add spicy or sweet 'bombs' to vary the flavor. Skip the edamame. (☎ 512-893-5561; www.ramen-tatsuya.com; 1234 S Lamar Blvd; ramen $10; ◷ 11am-10pm)

Tacodeli TEX-MEX $

12 ❌ MAP P74, B1

Oh Tacodeli, how we love your handcrafted tacos – surely blessed with the smiles of angels. From the Tacoloco with its adobo-braised brisket to the Pollo Fantastico with its shredded chicken and crema Mexican, the tacos are fresh, local and a touch gourmet. And you simply can't leave without trying the self-serve creamy dona sauce – it has kick. Order at the counter.

Across the street you can pick up the greenbelt trail for a nice stroll after lunch. (☎ 512-732-0303; www.tacodeli.com; 1500 Spyglass Dr; ◷ 7am-3pm Mon-Fri, 8am-3pm Sat & Sun)

Bouldin Creek Coffee House VEGETARIAN $

13 ❌ MAP P74, E5

You can get your veggie chorizo tacos or a potato leek omelet all day long at this buzzing vegan-vegetarian eatery. It's got an eclectic South Austin vibe and is a great place for people-watching, finishing your novel or joining a band. (☎ 512-416-1601; www.bouldincreekcafe.com; 1900 S 1st St; mains $6-10; ◷ 7am-midnight Mon-Fri, 8am-midnight Sat & Sun; 🛜 ✍)

Food Culture

Debating tacos There's no better way to start a conversation than to ask a local which restaurant serves the best tacos. Two perennial favorites are Torchy's Tacos (p80) and Tacodeli (p80). Torchy's has the mouthwatering fillings while Tacodeli brings it home with its dona sauce. In our opinion, a taste test is a win-win situation.

Late-night munchies For a cheap eats late at night, head to the takeout window at long-time favorite Home Slice (p80) for, well, a slice to take home. Or eat on the sidewalk.

Home Slice

PIZZA $

14 🗙 MAP P74, G4

Everybody knows about Home Slice. And on Saturday night between 6pm and midnight, it seems everybody is in fact here! All of them digging into the New York–style pies. If you're heading to a show, step into the darkly lit restaurant beforehand for a glass of wine with your pizza. If it's after the show, step up to the to-go window next door. (📞512-444-7437; www.homeslicepizza.com; 1415 S Congress Ave; slice $4, pizzas $15-22; ⏰11am-11pm Sun, Mon, Wed & Thu, to midnight Fri & Sat, to-go window 11am-11pm Sunday to Thursday, to 3am Sat & Sun)

Torchy's Tacos

TEX-MEX $

15 🗙 MAP P74, F4

At the South Austin Trailer Park location, they'll tell you what you should be ordering if they think you're making the wrong choice. We like your initiative Torchy's! This longtime favorite, which now has brick-and-mortar locations across the state, was former president Obama's pick on a 2016 Austin visit. His tacos of choice? The Democrat, the Republican and the Independent, we hear. (📞512-916-9235; www.torchystacos.com; 1311 S 1st St; tacos $3-5; ⏰7am-10pm Mon-Thu, 7am-11pm Fri, 8am-11pm Sat, 8am-10pm Sun)

Torchy's Tacos

JOSIAH TRUE/SHUTTERSTOCK ©

Whip In

INDIAN $

16 ⊗ MAP P74, H6

It started as a convenience store on a frontage road. Then the beer and Indian food started to take over. Now it's part Indian restaurant, part bar and part beer store, with a few groceries still hanging around to keep it confusing. Would we mention it if the food (breakfast naan and 'panaani' sandwiches) wasn't awesome? We would not. (☏512-442-5337; www.whipin.com; 1950 S I-35; breakfast $7-9, brunch, lunch & dinner $9-14; ⊙10am-11pm Sun-Mon, to midnight Tue-Sat)

Güero's Taco Bar

TEX-MEX $$

17 ⊗ MAP P74, G4

Set in a sprawling former feed-and-seed store from the late 1800s, this Austin classic always draws a crowd. Güero's may not serve the best Tex-Mex in town, but with its free chips and salsa, refreshing margaritas and convivial vibe, we can almost guarantee a fantastic time. And the food? Try the homemade corn tortillas and chicken tortilla soup.

Head to the oak-shaded garden for live music Wednesday through Sunday. (☏512-447-7688; www.gueros.com; 1412 S Congress Ave; breakfast $5-7, lunch & dinner $9-38; ⊙11am-10pm Mon-Wed, to 11pm Thu & Fri, 8am-11pm Sat, to 10pm Sun; ⊚)

A Congress Ave Alternative

If you tire of the crowds on S Congress Ave, take a walk or drive to nearby S 1st St. This burgeoning strip is filling up quickly with coffee shops and indie-owned eateries that rival their better-known neighbors in quality and style. For coffee, give scrappy Bouldin Creek Coffee House (p79) a try. Elizabeth Street Cafe is another great stop, where you can pick up French pastries or tasty banh mi.

Elizabeth Street Cafe

FRENCH, VIETNAMESE $$

18 ⊗ MAP P74, F4

We're going to irritate some locals by highlighting this dapper cottage of deliciousness. Pop in for croissants, crepes and a few noodle dishes in the morning, plus the deliciously creamy Vietnamese coffee. And the banh mi? Available all day, these soft baguettes are loaded with bewitchingly tasty fillings. Later in the day look for pho, bun and more Vietnamese house specialties. (☏512-291-2882; www.elizabethstreetcafe.com; 1501 S 1st St; pastries $2-7, breakfast $8-19, lunch & dinner $9-23; ⊙8am-10:30pm Sun-Thu, to 11pm Fri & Sat)

Uchi   JAPANESE $$$

19 ❌ MAP P74, E3

East and West collide beautifully at this top-notch South Austin sushi joint run by owner and executive chef Tyson Cole. The sleek interior would feel right at home in LA, and the sushi is every bit as fresh and imaginative as what you'd get there. (☏512-916-4808; www. uchiaustin.com; 801 S Lamar Blvd; sushi & small plates $3-22, sushi rolls $10-13; ⏱5-10pm Sun-Thu, to 11pm Fri & Sat)

Drinking

ABGB   BEER GARDEN

20 🔘 MAP P74, C5

Want a place to meet your friends for beer and conversation? Then settle in at a picnic table inside or out at this convivial brewery and beer garden that's also known for its great food. The boar, tasso and spinach pizza? Oh yes, you do want a slice of this thin-crusted specialty pie ($4). Live music Tuesday and Wednesday, and Friday through Sunday. Got Fido? He's welcome to join you. (Austin Beer Garden Brewery; ☏512-298-2242; www.theabgb.com; 1305 W Oltorf St; ⏱11:30am-11pm Tue-Thu, 11:30am-midnight Fri, noon-midnight Sat, noon-10pm Sun; 🛜🐾)

Hotel San José   BAR

21 🔘 MAP P74, G4

Transcending the hotel-bar genre, this is actually a cool, Zen-like outdoor patio that attracts a chill crowd, and it's a nice place to hang if you want to actually have a conversation. Service can be leisurely, but maybe that's OK for an oasis? (☏512-852-2350; 1316 S Congress Ave; ⏱noon-midnight)

Jo's Coffee   COFFEE

22 🔘 MAP P74, G4

Walk-up window, friendly staff, shaded patio, plus great people-watching... Throw in breakfast tacos, gourmet deli sandwiches and coffee drinks. Stick it in the middle of hopping South Congress, and you've got a classic Austin hangout. Don't miss the *I Love You So Much* mural (p76) on the north side. (☏512-444-3800; www.joscoffee.com; 1300 S Congress Ave; ⏱7am-9pm; 🛜)

Entertainment

Broken Spoke LIVE MUSIC

23 MAP P74, A5

George Strait once hung from the wagon-wheel chandeliers at the wooden-floored Broken Spoke, a true Texas honky-tonk. Not sure of your dance moves? Join a lesson, offered from 8pm to 9pm ($8). As the sign inside says: 'Please do Not!!!! Stand on the Dance Floor.' (512-442-6189; www.brokenspokeaustintx.net; 3201 S Lamar Blvd; 4-11:30pm Tue, to midnight Wed & Thu, 11am-1:30am Fri & Sat)

Continental Club LIVE MUSIC

24 MAP P74, G4

No passive toe-tapping here; the dance floor at this 1950s-era lounge is always swinging with some of the city's best local acts. On most Monday nights you can catch local legend Dale Watson and his Lone Stars (10:15pm). (512-441-2444; www.continentalclub.com; 1315 S Congress Ave; 4pm-2am Mon-Fri, from 1pm Sat, from 3pm Sun)

Alamo Drafthouse Cinema – S Lamar Blvd CINEMA

25 MAP P74, D3

Like the other outposts of this Austin-based movie chain, the focus is on the movie-going

Broken Spoke

experience. Reserved seating. No latecomers. No talking or texting. Just pure movie enjoyment. Food and alcohol served. (📞512-861-7040; www.drafthouse.com; 1120 S Lamar Blvd; movies $10.75-14.75)

Long Center for the Performing Arts   PERFORMING ARTS

26 ⭐ MAP P74, F2

This state-of-the-art theater opened in late 2008 as part of a waterfront redevelopment along Lady Bird Lake. The multistage venue hosts drama, dance, concerts and comedians. Also known for its gorgeous view of the downtown skyline from its outdoor terrace. (📞512-457-5100; www.thelongcenter.org; 701 W Riverside Dr)

Broken Spoke

When you're feeling ready for a little Texas two-steppin', there's only one place you should dream of going: the Broken Spoke (p83). This is honky-tonk heaven – a totally authentic Texas dance hall that's been in business since 1964. Here you'll find dudes in boots and Wranglers two-stepping around a crowded dance floor alongside hipsters, college students and slackers; it's one of the great, essential Austin experiences. (You'll know you've arrived when you spot a big old oak tree propping up an old wagon wheel out front.)

Saxon Pub   LIVE MUSIC

27 ⭐ MAP P74, D3

The super-chill Saxon Pub, presided over by 'Rusty,' a huge knight who sits out the front, has music every night, mostly Texas performers in the blues-rock vein. A great place to kick back, drink a beer and discover a new favorite artist. (📞512-448-2552; www.thesaxonpub.com; 1320 S Lamar Blvd)

Emo's East   LIVE MUSIC

28 ⭐ MAP P74, H4

For over 20 years, Emo's led the pack in the punk and indie scene in a crowded space on Red River St. Since 2011, it's been enjoying some shiny new digs (and a whole lot more space) out on Riverside. (📞tickets 888-512-7469; www.emosaustin.com; 2015 E Riverside Dr; ⏰showtimes vary)

Shopping

Austin Art Garage   ART

29 🔒 MAP P74, B5

This cool little independent...well, we hesitate to call it a 'gallery' because that would needlessly scare some people off. Anyway, it features some pretty great artwork by Austin artists. (Hey, Joel Ganucheau: we're fans.) Check out the website to catch the vibe, and definitely check out the 'gallery' if you like what you see. (📞512-351-5934; www.austinartgarage.com; 2200 S Lamar Blvd; ⏰11am-6pm Tue-Sun)

Bat Conservation International

Bat Conservation International (BCI; www.batcon.org) is based in Austin. Its mission? To conserve the world's bats and their ecosystems in order to keep the planet healthy. Visit the website for more information about bats worldwide and for updates about weather and bat viewing times in Austin. During summer viewing season, BCI volunteers share information about Austin's bats with visitors on the bridge (7pm to 9pm Thursday to Sunday).

Lucy in Disguise   VINTAGE

30 🔒 MAP P74, F4

Colorful and over the top, this South Congress staple has been outfitting Austinites for years. You can rent or buy costume pieces, which is this place's specialty, but you can also find everyday vintage duds as well. (📞512-444-2002; www.lucyindisguise. com; 1506 S Congress Ave; ⏲11am-7pm Mon-Thu, to 8pm Fri-Sun)

Stag   CLOTHING

31 🔒 MAP P74, G4

Embrace the art of manliness at this stylish SoCo store that's just for the guys, or for girls who are shopping for guys. (📞512-373-7824; www.stagaustin.com; 1423 S Congress Ave; ⏲11am-7pm Mon-Thu, to 8pm Fri & Sat, to 6pm Sun)

Yard Dog   ART

32 🔒 MAP P74, F5

Stop into this small but scrappy gallery that focuses on folk and outsider art. (📞512-912-1613; www. yarddog.com; 1510 S Congress Ave; ⏲11am-5pm Mon-Fri, 11am-6pm Sat, noon-5pm Sun)

Birds Barbershop   COSMETICS

33 🔒 MAP P74, C5

Hippest haircut in town; buzzcut $15. Complimentary Shiner beer included with cut. (📞512-442-8800; www.birdsbarbershop.com; 2110 S Lamar Blvd; ⏲9am-8pm Mon-Fri, to 7pm Sat, 10am-6pm Sun)

Walking Tour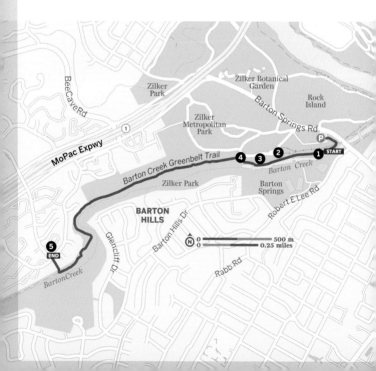

Urban Hike: Zilker Park & Barton Creek Greenbelt

Hundred-year-old Zilker Park is home to an entertaining mix of natural and constructed attractions. Many of the best are easily enjoyed near Barton Springs Pool. At the southwest end of the Barton Springs parking lot, you'll find the eastern trailhead to the 7.5-mile long Barton Creek Greenbelt.

Getting There

Car The Barton Springs parking lot is south of Barton Springs Rd.

Bike Two B-cycle stations near Barton Springs Pool.

Bus Barton Creek Greenbelt is served by the 30 bus.

❶ Hit the Water

Lakes, creeks and pools are what make **Zilker Park** (p68) special. To watch folks launching from shore into Barton Creek and paddlers on the water, walk to **Zilker Park Boat Rentals** (p69), which is tucked below the far eastern end of the Barton Springs Pool parking lot, downstream from the pool. This 45-year-old company rent canoes, kayaks and stand-up paddleboards.

❷ Family Fun

Just upstream kids enjoy the **playground**. A few steps away is the ticket office for the family-friendly **Zilker Zephyr** (☎512-478-8286; 2201 Barton Springs Rd; adult/child $3/2; ⏱10am-5pm). This open-air mini-train makes a 3-mile loop around the park on a 20- to 25-minute run.

❸ Barton Springs Pool

You'll find swimmers and waders enjoying this spring-fed **pool** (p69) year-round – about 600,000 annually they say. For a unique animal sighting, keep a lookout for the endangered Barton Springs salamander. This cold-blooded critter grows to a length of 2.5in and lives only in the four springs comprising Barton Springs. Plans are afoot – and growing more expensive – to create a 75ft-long waterway here as a new habitat for the salamander.

❹ Back to Nature

For a longer walk, hook up with the **Barton Creek Greenbelt** (p76). This well-used hiking and biking trail is dotted with swimming holes and limestone cliffs, the latter popular with rock climbers further along the trail. This is also the start of the Violet Crown Trail, which joins the greenbelt for about 4 miles. On the way to the next trailhead, you'll pass Campbell's Swimming Hole.

❺ Tacos & Trail Hiking

The next greenbelt access point after Zilker Park is 1500 Spyglass Rd, about 1.2 miles southwest of the Barton Springs entrance. This trailhead is actually closer to Campbell's Swimming Hole than Zilker Park. But perhaps the best part about the Spyglass trailhead is its proximity to **Tacodeli** (p79), known for its fast and tasty breakfast tacos. Stock up here. If you continue south on the greenbelt from the Spyglass trailhead, look for rock climbers.

Explore ◈

UT & Central Austin

The University of Texas (UT) cuts a huge swath across the city just north of downtown; look for the main tower and you'll know you've arrived. Even if you're not an alum or a UT Longhorn at heart, the campus is a pleasant place to stroll. It's also home to several worthwhile museums, although it's a long walk if you want to cover them all in one visit.

The Short List

○ *Harry Ransom Humanities Research Center (p93)* Pondering over a rare Gutenberg Bible.

○ *Lyndon Baines Johnson (LBJ) Library & Museum (p90)* Realizing the vast impact of the social programs supported by LBJ.

○ *Scholz Garten (p98)* Savoring a beer and appreciating the surroundings in a 150-year-old Biergarten.

○ *Elizabet Ney Museum (p96)* Striking a pose beside the statues in the studio of an acclaimed sculptor.

Getting There & Around

🚲 There is a B-cycle station at the corner of Congress Ave and E Martin Luther King Jr Blvd.

🚌 Bus 1, 10 or 142 from downtown.

UT & Central Austin Map on p94

UT Tower (p93) FIJPHOTO/SHUTTERSTOCK ©

Top Experience 📷

Look & Learn at Lyndon Baines Johnson (LBJ) Library & Museum

Engaging exhibits trace Johnson's rise to the presidency and focus on his most notable achievements. The man and his story come alive through important artifacts, recordings of his telephone conversations and life-size photos capturing significant or representative moments from his era.

◉ MAP P94, D6

📞 512-721-0200

www.lbjlibrary.org

2313 Red River St

adult/child 13-17yr $10/3

🕘 9am-5pm

Big Personality

The 36th president of the United States was a towering man with a big personality. Visitors can step up beside a life-size photo of the president to get the 'Johnson Treatment' – experiencing what it was like when the tall and imposing president (he was 6ft 3in) leaned close to emphasize a point. Nearby, an animatronic LBJ regales visitors with his recorded stories, highlighting the former president's skill at connecting with voters by emphasizing his homespun Texas roots.

November 22, 1963

Johnson became president of the United States on November 22, 1963, after his predecessor John F Kennedy was assassinated in Dallas. A moving exhibit spotlights various events on that tragic day and the days following. One large photograph shows Johnson taking the oath of office on Air Force One with his wife Lady Bird on one side and First Lady Jacqueline Kennedy on the other side. A letter from the First Lady to LBJ thanking him for his kindness and support is also displayed. You'll also see notes from Johnson's remarks at Andrews Air Force base later that day, his first address to the people as president.

Oval Office

Ride the elevator up to the 10th floor to see an exact replica of the Oval Office during Johnson's presidency. Well, almost exact. This one is 7/8ths of the room's actual size. Note the photograph of Johnson's presidential inspiration, Franklin Delano Roosevelt. Roosevelt appointed Johnson to be the Texas director of the National Youth Administration when Johnson was only in his twenties. The line-up of televisions is duplicated in Johnson's digs at the LBJ Ranch. One amusing artifact? Johnson's recorded phone conversation with Katharine Graham, publisher of the *Washington Post*. On this particular call, he lays on the charm pretty darn thick.

★ **Top Tip**

○ Parking lot 38 borders the sidewalk leading to the museum. It offers free parking, but the other lots beside it do not. Look for the banners at the entrance and double-check the signage.

✗ **Take a Break**

For lunch, head east from campus to Manor Rd, lined with fantastic restaurants. It's hard to go wrong with a taco from El Chilito (p59).

Top Experience 📷

Become a Longhorn for a Day at University of Texas at Austin

Whatever you do, don't call it 'Texas University' – them's fightin' words, usually used derisively by Texas A&M students to take their rivals down a notch. Sorry, A&M, but the main campus of the University of Texas is kind of a big deal. Established in 1883, UT has the largest enrollment in the state, with over 50,000 students.

◉ MAP P94, B6

www.utexas.edu

cnr University Ave & 24th St

Blanton Museum of Art

With one of the best university art collections in the USA, the **Blanton** (☑512-471-5482; www.blantonmuseum.org; 200 E Martin Luther King Jr Blvd; adult/child $9/free; ☉10am-5pm Tue-Fri, 11am-5pm Sat, 1-5pm Sun) showcases a variety of styles. It doesn't go very deeply into any of them, but then again you're bound to find something of interest. Especially striking is the permanent installation of *Missão/Missões (How to Build Cathedrals)* – which involves 600,000 pennies, 800 communion wafers and 2000 cattle bones.

Harry Ransom Humanities Research Center

The fascinating **Ransom Center** (☑512-471-8944; www.hrc.utexas.edu; 300 W 21st St; admission free; ☉10am-5pm Mon-Wed & Fri, to 7pm Thu, noon-5pm Sat & Sun) is a major repository of historic manuscripts, photography, books, film, TV, music and more. Highlights include a complete copy of the Gutenberg Bible (one of only five in the USA) and what is thought to be the first photograph ever taken, from 1826. Check the website for special online-only exhibitions and the center's busy events calendar of author readings, live music, lectures and more.

UT Tower

No building defines the campus as much as the UT Tower. Standing 307ft high, the tower looms large, both as a campus landmark and in Austin history as the perch that Charles Whitman used during a 1966 shooting spree. On a more cheerful note, it now serves as a beacon of victory when it's lit orange to celebrate a Longhorn win or other achievement.

The tower's observation deck is accessible only by **guided tour** (☑512-475-6636; https://tower.utexas.edu; $6; ☉hours vary). The tour includes an elevator ride to the 27th floor followed by a climb up three short flights of stairs (auxiliary elevator available for those with restricted mobility). Reserve your ticket in advance; pick it up at the Texas Union.

★ **Top Tips**

o Want to see some Big 12 football or other college athletics while you're in town? The **UT Box Office** (www.texassports.com; 2139 San Jacinto Blvd, Darrel K Royal-Texas Memorial Stadium) is your source for all things Longhorn.

o Admission is free on Thursdays at the Blanton Museum.

✕ **Take a Break**

The patio is the place to be for a coffee or beer at Spider House (p98).

Kick back with bratwurst and a beer in the festive Scholz Garten (p98).

UT & Central Austin Become a Longhorn for a Day at UT

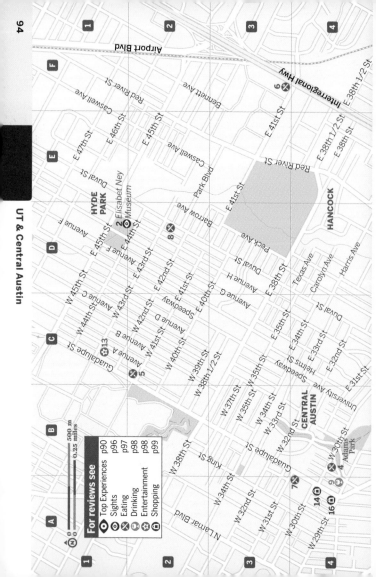

UT & Central Austin

Airport Blvd

HYDE PARK

HANCOCK

CENTRAL AUSTIN

For reviews see
◆ Top Experiences   p90
◎ Sights   p96
⊗ Eating   p97
◐ Drinking   p98
◔ Entertainment   p98
◎ Shopping   p99

500 m
0.25 miles

2 Elisabet Ney Museum

5

6

7

8

E 34th St

Werner Ave

Hollywood Ave

Robinson Ave

Edgewood Ave

CHERRYWOOD

E 31st St
E 32nd St
E 30th St
E 29th St
E 28th St

French Pl

Breeze Tce

Lafayette Ave

Manor Rd

E 22nd St

Chestnut Ave

Coledo St

Alamo
Pocket
Park

Poquito St

Chicon St

E 20th St

E 18th St

EAST
AUSTIN

E 16th St

E Martin Luther King Jr Blvd

Leona St

290

35

E Dean Keeton St

Mount
Calvary
Cemetery

Comal St

Duncan La

E 32nd St

Red River St

Medical Arts St

HANCOCK

Lyndon Baines (LBJ)
Library &
Museum

Trinity St

Red River St

Clyde Littlefield Dr

Interregional Hwy

Oakwood
Cemetery

D

E

F

E 32nd St

Harris Park Ave

Eastwoods
Neighborhood
Park

Robert Dedman Dr

E 30th St

E Dean Keeton St

Texas Memorial 3
Museum

E 23rd St

San Jacinto Blvd

Waller Creek

Red River St

12

Waterloo
Park

Trinity St

C

Speedway

W 27th St

University
of Texas
at Austin

East Mall

Speedway

E 21st St

E Martin Luther King Jr Blvd

E 18th St

E 17th St

E 16th St

10

Whitis Ave

Guadalupe St

11

University
of Texas
at Austin

W 24th St

West Mall
Inner Campus Cir

Hi, How Are
You Mural

15

1

University Ave

W 20th St

W Martin Luther King Jr Blvd

W 18th St

W 17th St

W 16th St

Guadalupe St

DOWNTOWN

B

Nueces St

W 26th St

Rio Grande St

W 22nd St

W 21st St

Lavaca St

W 15th St

Rio Grande St

A

Sights

Hi, How Are You Mural PUBLIC ART

1 MAP P94, A7

Created by songwriter and artist Daniel Johnston, this iconic bug-eyed frog greets passersby near the University of Texas. Also known as *Jeremiah the Innocent*, the mural covers the south wall of a Thai restaurant known as Thai, How Are You – which changed its name from the less pun-tastic Thai Spice. (cnr 21st & Guadalupe Sts)

Elisabet Ney Museum MUSEUM

2 MAP P94, D1

A German-born sculptor and spirited trailblazer, Elisabet Ney lived in Austin in the early 1880s, and her former studio is now one of the oldest museums in Texas. Filled with more than 100 works of art, including busts and statues of political figures, the castlelike building made from rough-hewn stone is reason enough to visit. Look for the hidden door on the 2nd floor. (☏512-974-1625; www.austintexas.gov/department/elisabet-ney-museum; 304 E 44th St; donations welcome; ☉noon-5pm Wed-Sun)

Texas Memorial Museum MUSEUM

3 MAP P94, C6

We all know how kids feel about dinosaurs, and this natural history museum is the perfect place for them to indulge their fascination. Look up to see the swooping skeleton of the Texas pterosaur – one of the most famous dino finds ever. This impressively humongous Cretaceous-era flying reptile has a wingspan of 40ft and was recovered at Big Bend in 1971. There are other exhibits, too, focusing on anthropology, natural history, geology and biodiversity. (☏512-471-1604; www.tmm.utexas.edu; 2400 Trinity St; adult/child $4/3; ☉9am-5pm Tue-Sat; 👪)

Civil Rights & Social Justice

Johnson spearheaded much of the social justice legislation passed in the 1960s, all part of his vision for a Great Society that would provide 'liberty and abundance for all.' The results of his efforts to reduce poverty, improve education and secure civil rights for all Americans live on today through the many programs he supported. The Social Justice Gallery in the Lyndon Baines Johnson (LBJ) Library & Museum (p90) discusses these different projects and programs, from civil rights to Medicare to public broadcasting and consumer protection. The civil rights exhibit displays the desk on which Johnson signed the Civil Rights Act of 1965.

Eating

Trudy's Texas Star   TEX-MEX $

4 MAP P94, B4

Get your Tex-Mex fix here; the menu is consistently good, with several healthier-than-usual options. But we'll let you in on a little secret: this place could serve nothing but beans and dirt and people would still line up for the margaritas, which might very well be the best in Austin. (📞512-477-2935; www.trudys.com; 409 W 30th St; breakfast $6-11, lunch & dinner $8-19; 🕐11am-2am Mon-Fri, from 9am Sat & Sun)

New World Deli   SANDWICHES $

5 MAP P94, C2

Fans of the sandwich will be delighted with the offerings at New World, whether they're after a sloppy joe, pastrami on rye, or curried chicken salad on wheat – all of which are made with New World's amazing, fresh-baked bread, and all of which will raise the bar on what you'll expect from any future sandwiches you encounter. (📞512-451-7170; www.newworlddeli.com; 4101 Guadalupe St; sandwiches $6-9; 🕐11am-9pm Mon-Sat, to 5pm Sun)

Freebirds World Burrito   MEXICAN $

6 MAP P94, F3

Burritos – and nothing but – are why you come to Freebirds. Each one is custom-made under your watchful eye, with a boggling

Texas Memorial Museum

number of combinations of tortilla, meat and toppings. For a place with kind of a rock-and-roll atmosphere, the staff is surprisingly friendly and helpful. (📞512-451-5514; www.freebirds.com; 1000 E 41st St; burritos under $10; 🕐10:30am-10pm Mon-Sat, to 9pm Sun)

Via 313   PIZZA $$

7 MAP P94, A4

What? Why is my pizza a square? Because it's Detroit-style, baby, meaning it's cooked in a square pan, plus there's caramelized cheese on the crust and sauce layered over the toppings. And after just one bite of one of these rich favorites, we guarantee you'll forget all geometric concerns. Good craft beer selection too. (📞512-358-6193; www.via313.com;

3016 Guadalupe St; pizzas $10-29;
⏲11am-11pm Sun-Thu, to 11pm Fri
& Sat)

Hyde Park
Bar & Grill
AMERICAN $$

8 ✗ MAP P94, D2

Look for the enormous fork out
front to guide you to this homey
neighborhood haunt. The diverse
menu has plenty of options, but no
matter what you choose, we insist
that you order the batter-dipped
French fries, which is what this
place is famous for. (☎512-458-
3168; www.hpbng.com; 4206 Duval
St; mains $8-19; ⏲11am-10:30pm
Mon-Thu, to 11pm Fri & Sat, 10:30am-
10:30pm Sun)

Drinking

Spider House
CAFE

9 ☕ MAP P94, A4

Traveling carnival? Haunted
house? Or a European cafe with
a great patio? North of campus,

Spider House has a big, funky
outdoor area bedecked with all
sorts of oddities. It's open late and
also serves beer and wine. In the
afternoon, bring a laptop, sip cof-
fee and use the wi-fi, available until
2am. (☎512-480-9562; 2908 Fruth
St; ⏲11am-2am; 🛜)

Scholz Garten
BEER HALL

10 🍺 MAP P94, C8

This German *biergarten* has been
around forever – or at least since
1866 – and its proximity to the
capitol building has made it the
traditional favorite of politicians.
The author O Henry was also a fan.
(☎512-474-1958; www.scholzgarten.
com; 1607 San Jacinto Blvd; ⏲11am-
10pm Mon-Sat, noon-8pm Sun)

Entertainment

Cactus Cafe
LIVE MUSIC

11 ⭐ MAP P94, B6

Listen to acoustic up close and
personal at this intimate club on
the UT campus. (www.cactuscafe.
org; Texas Union, cnr 24th & Guadalupe
Sts; ⏲showtimes vary)

Frank Erwin Center
STADIUM

12 ⭐ MAP P94, C8

This arena hosts big-name
concerts, UT men's and women's
basketball games, and graduation
ceremonies. (☎512-471-7744; www.
uterwincenter.com; 1701 Red River St)

Coffee
& Wi-fi

If you want to chill out over cof-
fee in a low-key and student-
friendly setting, head to the
eclectic Spider House, where
the table-filled patio is a great
spot for lounging and using
the wi-fi. Serves craft beer and
cocktails too.

Hyde Park Theatre   THEATER

13 ⭐ MAP P94, C1

This is one of Austin's coolest small theaters, presenting regional premieres of off-Broadway hits and recent Obie (Off-Broadway Theater Awards) winners. Its annual FronteraFest presents more than 100 new works over five weeks at venues around town. (☎512-479-7529; www.fronterafest. org; 511 W 43rd St)

Shopping

Antone's Records   MUSIC

14 🔒 MAP P94, A4

North of UT, legendary Antone's was founded in 1972 and has a well-respected selection of Austin, Texas and American blues music (with plenty of rare vinyl), plus a bulletin board for musicians, and vintage concert posters for sale. (☎512-322-0660; www.antones recordshop.com; 2928 Guadalupe St; ⏱10am-10pm Mon-Sat, 11am-8pm Sun)

University Co-op   GIFTS & SOUVENIRS

15 🔒 MAP P94, A6

Stock up on souvenirs sporting the Longhorn logo at this store

Student Life

Want to immerse in college culture? Then go where the students go. Step into the University Co-op for Longhorn mementos then stroll busy Guadalupe St, aka The Drag, on the western edge of the school. Interact with student guides on the UT Tower Tours (p93).

brimming with school spirit. It's amazing the sheer quantity of objects that come in burnt orange and white. (☎512-476-7211; www. universitycoop.com; 2246 Guadalupe St; ⏱9am-8pm Mon-Fri, to 7pm Sat, 11am-6pm Sun)

Buffalo Exchange   CLOTHING

16 🔒 MAP P94, A4

The Austin branch of this nation-wide used-clothing chain has an impressive selection of vintage clothes and shoes for men and women, including Texas styles and Western wear. (☎512-480-9922; 2904 Guadalupe St; ⏱10am-9pm Mon-Sat, 11am-8pm Sun)

Explore

Market District, Clarksville & North Austin

West of downtown, the Market District draws visitors to its large natural foods market and iconic stores. Compact Clarksville is one of the city's oldest neighborhoods. North Austin is largely residential but a few fantastic restaurants and bars add pizzazz. Just north of campus, Hyde Park was Austin's first suburb.

The Short List

○ **Little Longhorn Saloon (p110)** *Playing Chicken Shit Bingo and listening to country music.*

○ **Whole Foods Market (p106)** *Looping past the many food stalls trying to pick the perfect lunch.*

○ **Waterloo Records (p103)** *Checking out the list of recommended albums and maybe catching a live show.*

○ **Mean Eyed Cat (p110)** *Appreciating the Man in Black over beers.*

Getting There & Around

۶ There is a B-cycle station at W 5th St and Bowie St beside Whole Foods Market.

🚌 From downtown, bus 4, 21 and others will get you to the Market District. Bus 338 runs along Lamar Blvd, north and south of Lady Bird Lake.

🚗 The main road is N Lamar Ave, which runs north to south, eventually crossing Lady Bird Lake into South Austin. The western border is MoPac Expwy/Hwy Loop 1.

Neighborhood Map on p104

Whole Foods Market (p106)
CHRIS HOWES/WILD PLACES PHOTOGRAPHY/ALAMY STOCK PHOTO ©

Walking Tour 🥾

Market Stroll

Anchored by Whole Foods Market, the traffic-heavy Market District is a great spot for concentrated shopping, especially if you don't like malls. There's dedicated parking for the larger shops, and the market has become a social hub of sorts, with a wide selection of eateries inside and a lively patio beside the front parking lot.

Walk Facts

Start Whole Foods Market
End Duncan Park
Length 0.5 miles; 15 minutes

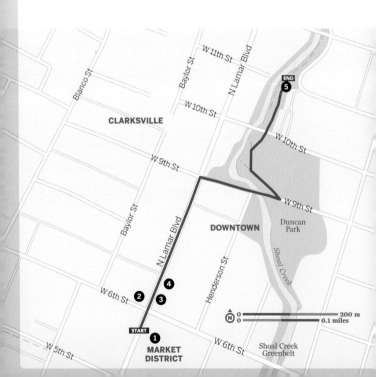

❶ Whole Day…in the Market

Open since 1980, this colossal **Whole Foods** (p106) is the flagship store for the nation-wide natural foods grocery chain. It's a bit of a zoo, but that's part of the fun. The craziness starts in the underground parking garage, where you might encounter an employee directing traffic. Inside are stations for tacos, sushi, coffee and more. On weekends, there's live music on the patio.

❷ Records Ain't Retro

Across W 6th St is beloved **Waterloo Records** (☎512-474-2500; www.waterloorecords.com; 600 N Lamar Blvd; ⏱10am-11pm Mon-Sat, from 11am Sun), which opened in 1982. The store is spacious and well-stocked. Come here to buy or sell new and used vinyl, CDs and DVDs. Texas artists are well represented in the inventory. Look for in-store performances. The best part may be the helpful and welcoming service – no old-school record-store snobs here.

❸ Gear Up for the Outdoors

To buy last-minute hiking and backpacking equipment before heading out to Big Bend National Park, step inside **REI** (601 N Lamar Blvd; www.rei.com) across the street from Waterloo. It also sells clothing, footwear, and books and maps.

❹ Bookworm Paradise

If you're into books, **BookPeople** (☎512-472-5050; 603 N Lamar Blvd; ⏱9am-11pm) feels like an old friend. As you wander the stacks, you'll notice detailed staff recommendations beneath the packed-tight shelves. There's a strong travel section in back. The store holds more than 300 book signings per year, so there's likely somebody of interest in-house on any given week. If you've got younger kids, stop by for story time at 11:30am on Saturdays. Take a break at the cafe, which serves coffee, sandwiches and desserts.

❺ Walk in the Park

To finish your exploration in natural surroundings, take a stroll alongside Shoal Creek in **Duncan Park**.

A B C D

1

🔒 15

N 0 ———— 200 m
0 ———— 0.1 m

MoPac Expwy

Newfield La

W 8th St

W 10th St

W 12th St

W 11 1/2 St

W 9th 1/2 St

W11th St

Eason St

W 10th St

Elm St

2

Theresa Ave

Patterson Ave

Augusta Ave

Campbell St

W 9th St

W Lynn St

W 9th St

CLARKSVILLE

W6th St

W8th St

3

W 5th St

11 📷

W Lynn St

W 6th St

12 ⭐

Highland Ave

Oakland Ave

Pressler St

Powell St

Paul St

4

North Austin

0 ———— 2 km
0 ———— 1 mile

Shoal Creek

Justin La

7 ✪

6 ✖

N Lamar Blvd

St Johns Ave

W 5th St

Orchard St

W4th St

5

Scoot Creek Blvd

10 🏠

Koenig La

9 📷

Hancock Dr

Burnet Rd

W North Loop Blvd

13 🔒

N Lamar Blvd

Airport Blvd

Interregional Hwy

W Cesar Chavez St (W 1st St)

MoPac Expwy

W 45th St

NORTH
AUSTIN

5 📷

3 ✖

N Lamar Blvd

E 45th St

Duval St

E 51st St

14 🔒

6

See Main Map
(1.6mi)

W 38th St

35

Lady Bird
Lake

A B C D

Market District, Clarksville & North Austin

E   F   G   H

Enfield Rd

See North Austin
Inset (1.6mi)

For reviews see
⊙	Sights	p106
✗	Eating	p106
🍷	Drinking	p110
★	Entertainment	p110
🔒	Shopping	p110

W 13th St

Maufrais St
Lorraine St
Shelley Ave
W 12th St
Windsor Rd
Castle Hill St
Parkway
Baylor St

House
Park

West Ave

W 10th St
W 9 1/2 St
West Austin
Neighborhood
Park

Castle Hill
Fitness
1⊙

W 11th St

W 12th St

Nelson St
W 9th St
W 10th St
Baylor St
W 11th St
N Lamar Blvd

8✗

W 11th St

Hartham St
Blanco St
W 8th St
W 7th St
Baylor St

Duncan
Park

West Ave

W 10th St

W 9th St

Rio Grande St

W 8th St

Walsh St
W 6th St

✗2

Henderson St
Wood St
Shoal Creek

DOWNTOWN

W 7th St

Baylor St
N Lamar Blvd

✗4

MARKET
DISTRICT

Bowie St

West Ave

W 6th St

W 5th St

Nueces St

Amtrak
Station
W 3rd St

W 3rd St

Shoal Creek
Greenbelt

W 4th St

P

E   F   G   H

Sights

Castle Hill Fitness

GYM

1 ◎ MAP P104, G2

The focus here is on classes and fitness machines. Check out the website for information on super-affordable two-week memberships or 10-visit passes. (☎512-478-4567; www.castlehillfitness.com; 1112 N Lamar Blvd; ⏲5:30am-10pm Mon-Thu, to 9pm Fri, 8am-7pm Sat & Sun)

Eating

Amy's Ice Creams

ICE CREAM $

2 ✖ MAP P104, F4

It's not just the ice cream we love; it's the toppings that get pounded and blended in, violently but lovingly, by the staff wielding a metal scoop in each hand. Amy's has other locations around Austin, too: you can find it on Guadalupe St north of the UT campus, on South Congress, or at Austin-Bergstrom

Airport. (☎512-480-0673; www.amysicecreams.com; 1012 W 6th St; ice cream $3.25-6; ⏲11:30am-midnight Sun-Thu, to 1am Fri & Sat)

Uchiko

JAPANESE $$$

3 ✖ MAP P104, B6

Not content to rest on his Uchi laurels, chef Tyson Cole opened this bustling North Lamar restaurant, which describes itself as 'Japanese farmhouse dining.' All we can say is, if these fantastic and unique delicacies are anything to go by, you'll soon be yearning to visit a few Japanese farmhouses. Reservations are highly recommended. (☎512-916-4808; www.uchikoaustin.com; 4200 N Lamar Blvd; small plates $4-28, sushi rolls $10-16; ⏲5-10pm Sun-Thu, to 11pm Fri & Sat)

Whole Foods Market

MARKET $

4 ✖ MAP P104, F5

The flagship of the Austin-founded Whole Foods Market is a gourmet grocery and cafe with restaurant counters and a staggering takeaway buffet, including self-made salads, global mains, deli sandwiches and more. The sushi tuna burritos ($11) from the sushi counter are delicious.

If there's no parking in the lot out front, head to the free underground garage. (www.wholefoods.com; 525 N Lamar Blvd; sandwiches $6-9, mains $6-15; ⏲7am-10pm; 📶)

Neighborhood Dining

If you just stick to the buzziest restaurants, you'll miss some fantastic neighborhood stand-bys, from the hearty breakfasts at Kerbey Lane Café (p108) to the beloved Mexican dishes of Fonda San Miguel (p109), to the dinners at night-out favorite Wink (p109).

Amy's Ice Creams

Whole Foods Market

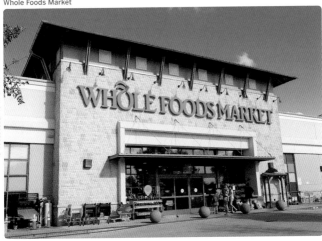

Kerbey Lane Café

AMERICAN $

5 🍴 MAP P104, A6

Kerbey Lane is a longtime Austin favorite, fulfilling round-the-clock cravings for anything from gingerbread pancakes to black-bean tacos to mahimahi. Try the addictive Kerbey Queso while you wait. (They have vegan queso, too!) There are several other locations around town, but this one in a homey bungalow is the original and has the most character. (📞512-451-1436; www.kerbeylanecafe. com; 3704 Kerbey Lane; breakfast $6-13, lunch & dinner $9-13; ⏱6:30am-11pm Mon-Thu, 24hr from 6:30am Fri-11pm Sun; 🍴👶)

Stiles Switch

BARBECUE $

6 🍴 MAP P104, B5

With manageable lines, you won't have to suffer to enjoy outstanding brisket, fired up to tender, smoky perfection, at this popular eatery 6 miles north of downtown. Top it off with some ribs, a side of corn casserole and a local microbrew. (📞512-380-9199; www.stilesswitch bbq.com; 6610 N Lamar Blvd; mains $7-18; ⏱11am-9pm Tue-Thu, to 10pm Fri & Sat, to 9pm Sun)

Barley Swine

AMERICAN $$$

7 🍴 MAP P104, B4

Small plates. Tantalizing flavors. Locally sourced. Changing menus. Snout-to-tail culinary creations. And craft cocktails. All served

Little Longhorn Saloon (p110)

I Scream, You Scream

Short of jumping into Barton Springs, there's no better way to cool off than at Amy's Ice Creams (p106). It's not just the ice cream itself, which, by the way, is smooth, creamy and delightful. It's the toppings – pardon us, *crush'ns* they call 'em – that get pounded and blended in, violently but lovingly, by staff wielding a metal scoop in each hand. Mexican vanilla bean with fresh strawberries, dark chocolate with Reese's Peanut Butter Cups, or mango with jelly beans if that's what you're into. With 15 flavors (rotated from their 300 recipes) and dozens of toppings, ranging from cookies and candy, to fruit or nuts, the combinations aren't endless, but they number too high to count. Look for other locations on Guadalupe St north of the UT campus, on South Congress near all the shops, or at the airport for a last-ditch fix.

in a rustically chic setting. Yep, hardcore farm-to-table joints are trending these days, but Barley Swine has a sense of fun often missing from similar establishments. Why yes, I will have the Rotating Obligatory Tiki – only $6 during the Swine Time happy hour (4pm to 7pm Monday to Friday). (☏512-394-8150; www.barleyswine. com; 6555 Burnet Rd; small plates $9-30; ☺5-10pm Sun-Thu, to 11pm Fri & Sat)

Wink FUSION $$$

8 ✖ MAP P104, G3

Date night? At this intimate gem hidden behind Whole Earth Provision Co, diners are ushered to tables underneath windows screened with Japanese rice paper, then presented with an exceptional wine list. The chef-inspired fare takes on a nouveau fusion attitude that is equal parts modern French and Asian. For a special splurge, try the five-course ($68) tasting menu. (☏512-482-8868; 1014 N Lamar Blvd; mains $17-33; ☺6-9:30pm Mon-Wed, 5:30-9:30pm Thu-Sat)

Fonda San Miguel MEXICAN $$$

9 ✖ MAP P104, B5

The gorgeous building is drenched in the atmosphere of old Mexico, with folk-inspired art, and it's been serving interior Mexican cooking for over 25 years. The Sunday brunch buffet is an impressive event but, at $39 per person, you'd better come hungry to make it worthwhile. Note that the last seating is one hour before close. (☏512-459-4121; 2330 W North Loop Blvd; mains $16-39; ☺5:30-9:30pm Mon-Thu, to 10:30pm Fri & Sat, 11am-2pm Sun)

Drinking

Little Longhorn Saloon
BAR

10 MAP P104, B5

This funky little cinder-block building, 5 miles north of downtown, is one of those dive bars that Austinites love so very much. They did even before it became nationally famous for Chicken Shit Bingo on Sunday night, when it's so crowded you can barely see the darn chicken – but, hey, it's still fun. There's live music most other nights. (www.thelittlelonghornsaloon. com; 5434 Burnet Rd; ☉5pm-midnight Tue & Wed, to 1am Thu-Sat, 2-10pm Sun)

Live in Austin

You don't have to head to a club or performance hall for great live entertainment. There's free live music regularly at Whole Foods Market (p106) and Waterloo Records (p103), as well as frequent author appearances at Book-People Inc (p103).

Austin's freak flag flies during **Eeyore's Birthday Party** (☎512-448-5160; www.eeyores. com; Pease Park, 1100 Kingsbury St; ☉late Apr; 🚼) in late April, when maypole dancing and genial weirdness reign for the day.

Mean Eyed Cat
BAR

11 MAP P104, B3

We're not sure if this watering hole is a legit dive bar or a calculated dive bar (it opened in 2004). Either way, a bar dedicated to Johnny Cash has our utmost respect. Inside this former chainsaw repair shop, Man in Black album covers, show posters and other knickknackery adorn the walls. A 300-year-old live oak anchors the lively patio. (☎512-920-6645; www. themeaneyedcat.com; 1621 W 5th St; ☉11am-2am)

Entertainment

Donn's Depot
LIVE MUSIC

12 ⭐ MAP P104, C4

Austin loves a dive bar, and Donn's combines a retro atmosphere inside an old railway car with live music six nights a week, including Donn himself performing alongside the Station Masters. A mix of young and old come to Donn's, and the dance floor sees plenty of action. (☎512-478-0336; www.donnsdepot.com; 1600 W 5th St; ☉2pm-2am Mon-Fri, from 6pm Sat)

Shopping

Blue Velvet
VINTAGE

13 🔒 MAP P104, B5

Western wear, vintage T-shirts and even oddities such as all-American bowling wear hang on the racks at Blue Velvet, where

Uchiko
Sake Social

Stylish Uchiko (p106) is lauded by locals for its fresh and exquisitely flavored sushi and seafood dishes. But prices are steep, reflecting the high quality of the fare. On a budget? Don't despair, just eat early. To sample the food at wallet- and purse-friendly prices, visit during the **Sake Social** happy hour, held nightly (5pm to 6:30pm). Several rolls are $6, while a half-dozen small bites under $7 offer a broad sampling of the menu. Sake, beer and wine selections range from $3 to $7.

you'll find an equal number of men and women eyeing the goods. Summer fashions are stocked year-round. (📞512-452-2583; www.bluevelvetaustin.com; 217 W North Loop Blvd; ⏱11am-8pm Mon-Sat, to 7pm Sun)

New Bohemia   JEWELRY

14 🔒 MAP P104, C6

When it comes to retro thrift shops, New Bohemia is the place to look for vintage jewelry and clothing. (📞512-326-1238; www.facebook.com/newbohemiaatx; 4631 Airport Blvd; ⏱noon-9pm)

Domain   MALL

15 🔒 MAP P104, B1

Stores like Apple, Neiman Marcus and Anthropologie line the streets of this upscale outdoor mall in far northwest Austin. (📞512-795-4230; www.simon.com/mall/the-domain; 11410 Century Oaks Tce; ⏱10am-9pm Mon-Sat, noon-6pm Sun)

Explore
West Austin

For outdoor recreation beyond Lady Bird Lake, plus a few scenic places to relax and enjoy the afternoon, head west. Parks along Lake Austin draw hikers and nature lovers, while Hamilton Pool Preserve is a gorgeous spot for a refreshing dip. Dripping Springs is the gateway to the Hill Country and keeps Austin day-trippers happy with wineries, microbreweries, distilleries and great restaurants.

The Short List

○ **Mt Bonnell (p114)** *Climbing the steps to the top of Austin's highest point to watch the sunset.*

○ **Hamilton Pool Preserve (p120)** *Taking a refreshing swim in a lush natural pool surrounded by limestone cliffs.*

○ **Lady Bird Lake (p120)** *Paddling across still waters in a kayak on a warm afternoon.*

○ **Jester King Brewery (p122)** *Sampling sour beers beneath leafy oaks on a lazy Saturday in Dripping Springs.*

○ **Salt Lick (p121)** *Digging into delicious barbecue cooked on outdoor fire pits.*

Getting There & Around

🚗 To get to Mt Bonnell, follow W 35th St west to Mt Bonnell Rd. To drive to Dripping Springs, follow Hwy 290 W.

West Austin Map on p118

Top Experience 📷
Climb the 102 Steps of Mt Bonnell

On weekends you might find yourself tip-toeing around a wedding ceremony atop Mt Bonnell, the highest point in the city at 775ft. This pretty overlook has impressed day-trippers since the 19th century. At sunset, climb the short but steep stairway for broad views of Lake Austin, the homes along the nearby hillsides and the Hill Country.

◉ MAP P118, F1

Covert Park

☎ 512-974-6700

www.austintexas.gov

3800 Mt Bonnell Rd

History of the Hill

The first recorded mention of Mt Bonnell appeared in 1839 when Albert Sidney Johnson, the Secretary of War for the Republic of Texas, mentioned it in correspondence. Johnson was there to defend the new capital of Austin, and this high viewpoint overlooking the Colorado River was critical for military defense purposes. In subsequent years, as the threat of Native American and Mexican attacks subsided, Mt Bonnell became a favorite spot for sightseers. Major General George Custer picnicked atop Mt Bonnell with his wife Elizabeth after the Civil War. In her book *Tenting on the Plains* she remarked upon the fine views and the steepness of the climb.

Just the Facts

Mt Bonnell is located within Covert Park. The climb from the parking lot to the top of the peak is 102 steps. There's a view deck at the summit, plus a historic marker, but don't stop here. Follow the short trails north and south for a variety of views – and the perfect picnic spot. Lake Austin, visible below, was created after the completion of the Tom Miller Dam in 1940 on the Colorado River.

What's in a Name?

According to the historic marker, Mt Bonnell was named for George Bonnell, a commissioner of Indian Affairs for the Texas Republic. The West Point Society, however, has long believed that the peak was originally named for Joseph Bonnell, a West Point graduate and Texas military hero. The West Point Society filed a suit with the 3rd Court of Appeals in Austin arguing that the Texas State Historical Survey Commission erred when it decided in 1969 that the peak had been named – back in the 1800s – for George Bonnell. The court took a look at the old dusty history and the lack of primary records from the time and decided it was a matter best left to the executive branch or the legislature.

★ **Top Tip**

◦ No parking in the lot at the base of Mt Bonnell from 10pm to 5am.

✕ **Take a Break**

Fuel up with a hearty Tex-Mex breakfast at Magnolia Cafe (p122).

After a late-morning climb to the summit, drive west to Dripping Springs for pizza and craft beer at Jester King Brewery (p122).

West Austin Climb the 102 Steps of Mt Bonnell

Walking Tour 🥾

Exploring Lady Bird Lake

The city christened the trails encircling Lady Bird Lake the Ann & Roy Butler Hike-and-Bike Trail in 2011, named for an involved former mayor and his wife. A few years later, a full 10.1-mile trail around the lake was completed and several new features – from a lakeside boardwalk to artsy restrooms – were introduced to the jogging and cycling masses. And we mean masses. The paths here experience 2.6 million visits per year.

Walk Facts

Start Deep Eddy Pool
End Boardwalks
Length 3.5 miles; 1½ hours

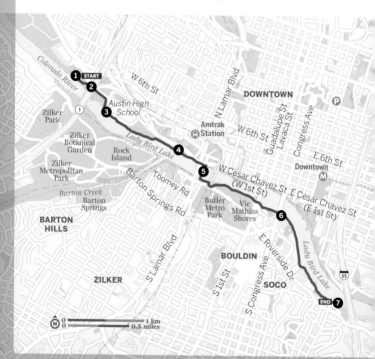

❶ Deep Eddy Pool

If you picture an overgrown natural swimming hole when you hear the name **Deep Eddy Pool** (p120), think again. This Austin landmark, like Barton Springs Pool across the lake, is a constructed outdoor swimming pool, complete with a lifeguard and lap swimmers. It is unique in that it is fed by cold natural springs. Deep Eddy is the oldest swimming pool in the state.

❷ Johnson Creek Trailhead

A crossroads awaits at the Johnson Creek Trailhead across from Austin High School. You can walk cross the lake and head toward the Austin Nature & Science Center (p69) and other Zilker Park attractions on the south side of the lake, or continue east. Helpful signage at the trailhead provides the mileage for various loops around the lake via different bridges.

❸ Texas Rowing Center

If the sight of all those folks paddling across the water inspires you to join them, stop by the lakeside **Texas Rowing Center** (www. texasrowingcenter.com), where you'll find kayaks, canoes and stand-up paddleboards for rent.

❹ Heron Creek Restrooms

The sleek Heron Creek Restrooms blend form and functionality along the trail.

❺ Pfluger Pedestrian Bridge

The Pfluger Pedestrian Bridge, also open to cyclists, connects downtown to Butler Park on the south side of the lake. The bridge opened in 2001 as an alternative to the nearby Lamar Boulevard Bridge, a narrow and heavily trafficked crossing point that was a dangerous route for walkers, joggers and cyclists.

❻ Austin Chronicle Building

From the lawn of the Austin Chronicle building near the Congress Avenue Bridge, stake out a spot to watch the colony of Mexican free-tailed bats stream out along the river to feed, best seen April through November.

❼ Boardwalks

A series of boardwalks stretch east for 1.1 miles along the river, offering stellar views of the downtown skyline.

✗ Take a Break

After your return to Deep Eddy Pool, make your way to the Mean Eyed Cat (p110), a welcoming neighborhood bar with an agreeable Johnny Cash obsession and a great patio.

West Austin

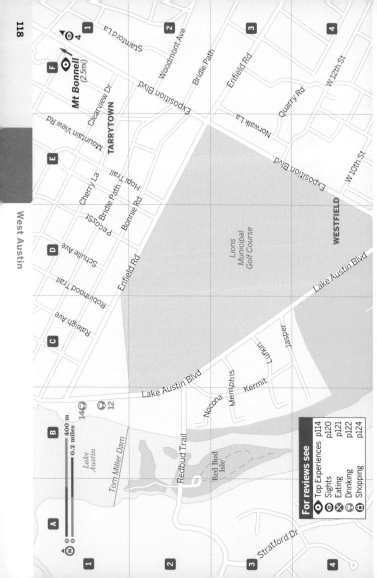

Lake Austin

TARRYTOWN

Mt Bonnell (2.5mi)

WESTFIELD

Lions
Municipal
Golf Course

Lake Austin Blvd

Lake Austin Blvd

Tom Miller Dam

Redbud Trail

Red Bud
Isle

Stratford Dr

Stamford La
Woodmont Ave
Bridle Path
Enfield Rd
W 12th St
Exposition Blvd
Clearview Dr
Mountain View Rd
Cherry La
Bridle Path
Pecos St
Bonnie Rd
Hopi Trail
Schulle Ave
Robinhood Trail
Raleigh Ave
Enfield Rd
Quarry Rd
Norwalk La
Exposition Blvd
W 10th St
Jasper
Lufkin
Kermit
Memphis
Nocona

400 m
0.2 miles

For reviews see
◆ Top Experiences p114
◎ Sights p120
✕ Eating p121
🍷 Drinking p122
🛍 Shopping p124

West Austin

Around Dripping Springs

See Around Dripping Springs Inset (10mi)

Main Map (10mi)

ROLLINGWOOD

BLUFFINGTON

Mopac Expwy

Veterans Dr

Veterans Park

Eilers Park

Deep Eddy Pool

Lady Bird Lake

Zilker Park

Colorado River

Lake Travis

Hamilton Pool Preserve

Barton Creek

Onion Creek

Dripping Springs

Meriden La
Atlanta St
Upson St
Deep Eddy Ave
Foster Ave
Hearn St
W 10th St
W 9th St
W 8th St
Pruett St
W 7th St
Norwalk La
Wayside Dr
Lake Austin Blvd

Stratford Dr
Vance La
Riley Rd
Hatley St
Yale St
Bettis Blvd

Stratford Dr
Ridgewood Rd

Hamilton Pool Rd
Fitzhugh Rd
McGregor La

71
71
12
150
290
290
1826
3238
12

13 ✕
7 ✕
3 ◎
1 ◎
15 ◉ 🚇

2 ◉
10 ℹ
9 ℹ
8 ◎
6 ✕
5 ✕
11 ✕

0 5 miles
0 10 km

Sights

Lady Bird Lake CANOEING

1 ◎ MAP P118, E8

Named after former First Lady 'Lady Bird' Johnson, Lady Bird Lake is actually a dammed-off section of the Colorado River. Get on the water at the rowing dock, which rents kayaks, stand-up paddleboards and canoes from $10 to $20 per hour Monday to Thursday, and slightly higher prices on weekends. (☏512-459-0999; www.rowingdock.com; 2418 Stratford Dr; ◷9am-8pm)

Hamilton Pool Preserve WATERFALL

2 ◎ MAP P118, A6

How gorgeous is the pool beneath Hamilton Creek, which spills over limestone outcroppings just upstream from the Pedernales River? Let's just say reservations are needed to visit this lush box canyon and waterfall-fed swimming hole from late spring through early fall. The special spot sits within a 30,428-acre preserve, which is also home to the endangered gold-cheeked warbler, a striking yellow-crowned bird.

The preserve can also fill up on winter weekends, before the spring and summer busy season, so get there early if the weather is looking nice. (☏512-264-2740; https://parks.traviscountytx.gov; 24300 Hamilton Pool Rd; per vehicle $15; ◷9am-6pm; reservations required May-Sep; Ⓟ)

Deep Eddy Pool SWIMMING

3 ◎ MAP P118, E7

Complete with vintage 1930s bathhouse, built by the Works Progress Administration, Texas' oldest swimming pool is fed by cold springs and surrounded by cottonwood trees. Separate areas accommodate waders and lap swimmers. (☏512-472-8546; www.deepeddy.org; 401 Deep Eddy Ave; adult/child under 11yr/12-17yr $9/5/4; ◷8am-10pm Mon-Fri, to 9pm Sat & Sun)

Mayfield House & Nature Preserve PARK

4 ◎ MAP P118, F1

Did somebody say peacocks? Kids will love gawking at these showy birds while exploring the riverside trails and grounds at this low-key park beside Lake

Outdoor Art Beside the Lake

To add to your climb up Mt Bonnell with eye-catching outdoor art, make your way to the Betty and Edward Marcus Sculpture Park at **Laguna Gloria** (3809 W 35th St; $5), the West Austin branch of Contemporary Austin (p42). Perfect for strolling, the sculpture-dotted grounds sprawl across 14 lush and woodsy acres beside Lake Austin. The sculpture park is open 9am to 5pm Monday through Saturday and from 10am to 5pm Sunday. Free admission on Tuesdays.

ROSCHETZKY PHOTOGRAPHY/SHUTTERSTOCK ©

Lady Bird Lake

Austin. The park is a nice companion to Mt Bonnell, just up the road, if you want to do a bit more hiking and exploring. It's a good place to let younger kids run a little bit wild. No pets. (☏512-974-6700; 3805 W 35th St; admission free; 🚸)

Eating

Salt Lick
BARBECUE $$

5 🍴 MAP P118, B8

It's worth the 20-mile drive out of town just to see the massive outdoor barbecue pits at this parklike place off Hwy 290. It's a bit of a tourist fave, but the crowd-filled experience still gets our nod. Hungry? Choose the family-style all-you-can-eat option (adult/ child $25/9). Cash only and BYOB. (☏512-858-4959; www.saltlickbbq.com; 18300 FM 1826, Driftwood; mains $10-22; ⏱11am-10pm; 🚸)

Pieous
PIZZA $

6 🍴 MAP P118, C7

Holy moly, this wood-fired pizza joint, in a strip mall 7 miles east of Dripping Springs – almost in Austin – serves good pie. Its motto, 'food is our religion,' gives a nod to its name, and to its focus on using fresh and homemade ingredients. The beloved pastrami is cooked in a BBQ smoker. (☏512-394-7041; www.facebook.com/pieous; 166 Hargraves Dr, Belterra Village; pizzas $10-16; ⏱11am-2pm & 4-9pm Mon-Fri, 11am-9pm Sat, to 8pm Sun; 🅿)

Magnolia Cafe TEX-MEX $

7 MAP P118, F7

In Westlake, opposite Deep Eddy Cabaret, this casual, all-night cafe serves American and Tex-Mex standbys such as *migas,* enchiladas, pancakes and potato scrambles. It gets absurdly crowded on weekends. (512-478-8645; www.themagnoliacafe.com; 2304 Lake Austin Blvd; breakfast $5-9, mains $7-16; 24hr)

Drinking

Jester King Brewery

8 MAP P118, B7 MICROBREWERY

Jester King may be the perfect country brewery. In a rural setting with picnic tables, cornhole games, shady oaks and a barn-style brewery, the backdrop is mighty picturesque, especially as the sun goes down. The long beer menu, with a focus on sour brews, is fun to sample. Hours may vary

A Drip by Any Other Name

Dripping Springs (p126) is juggling two nicknames these days, drawing road-trippers as the 'Gateway to the Hill Country' and impressing brides and grooms as the 'Wedding Capital of Texas.' And some locals have dubbed the place 'West of Weird,' a nod to folks keepin' it weird in Austin.

seasonally. (www.jesterkingbrewery.com; 13187 Fitzhugh Rd; 4-10pm Fri, noon-10pm Sat, noon-7pm Sun)

Treaty Oak Distilling DISTILLERY

9 MAP P118, B7

This destination distillery is the perfect host: fun, friendly and a master when it comes to cocktails. Sample its spirits in the tasting room then head to one of the bars for a fine mixed drink. You can supplement your sipping with snacks, a burger or a sandwich from the on-site **Ghost Hill Restaurant**. (512-599-0335; www.treatyoakdistilling.com; 16604 Fitzhugh Rd; restaurant snacks $2-10, mains $6-7; 3-9pm Fri, noon-9pm Sat, noon-6pm Sun)

Hawk's Shadow Winery WINERY

10 MAP P118, A7

This family-run winery is the full package: Texas hospitality, sweet views of the Hill Country from the patio and small-batch reds infused with Texas terroir – and that means easy drinking. Budding geologists can step into the cellar for a look at fossils found in the limestone here. (512-587-9085; www.hawksshadow.com; 7500 McGregor Lane; tasting per person $10; noon-6pm Sat, by appointment Wed-Fri & Sun;)

Twisted X Brewing Co MICROBREWERY

11 MAP P118, B8

Open a bit earlier than other local microbreweries, Twisted X is an

Hill Country Wineries

When most people think of Texas, they think of cowboys, cactus and Cadillacs – not grapes. But the Lone Star State is a major wine producer, and the Hill Country, with its robust Provence-like limestone and hot South African–style climate, has become the state's most productive wine-making region. Sitting a short drive west and south of Austin, the rolling hills of the Hill Country are home to more than 50 wineries, with the largest concentration of vineyards found around Fredericksburg, primarily along Hwy 290.

Most larger wineries are open daily for tastings and tours. Many also host special events, such as grape stompings and annual wine and food feasts. Smaller wineries are typically open during set hours on weekends, but by appointment on weekdays. Local visitor bureaus stock the handy *Texas Hill Country Wineries Guide & Map*, which summarizes the wineries and pinpoints their locations (or visit www.texaswinetrail.com).

You could leave the driving to someone else with **Fredericksburg Limo & Wine Tours** (📞830-992-0696; www.texaswinelimos.com; tours per person $109-149), which offers limo tours or more affordable shuttle van tours. For a list of tour operators, check www.wineroad290. com, which covers wineries along Hwy 290 and provides a map of their locations.

easygoing spot for a post-work drink. Ingredients from Texas and Mexico keep things regional. Try the tasty Fuego, which will kick your palate with a touch of jalapeño sass. (📞512-829-5823; www. twistedxbrewing.com; 23455 W RR 150; ⏰11am-9pm Thu-Sat, noon-8pm Sun)

Hula Hut BAR

12 📍 MAP P118, B1

The hula theme is so thorough that this restaurant feels like a chain, even though it's not. But the bar's sprawling deck that stretches out over Lake Austin makes it a popular hangout among Austin's nonslackers. (📞512-476-4852; 3825 Lake Austin Blvd; ⏰11am-10pm Mon-Thu, to 11pm Fri, 10:30am-11pm Sat, to 10pm Sun)

Deep Eddy Cabaret BAR

13 📍 MAP P118, E7

This great little neighborhood bar is known for its excellent jukebox, loaded with almost a thousand tunes in all genres. Yep, it's a dive, but a top-rate one. (📞512-472-0961; 2315 Lake Austin Blvd; ⏰noon-2am)

Scenic Drive: Wildflower Trails in the Hill Country

Thanks to former First Lady Claudia Taylor Johnson – around here everyone calls her Lady Bird – each spring the highways are lined with stunning wildflowers that stretch for miles, planted as part of her Highway Beautification Act.

You know spring has arrived in Texas when you see cars pulling up roadside and families climbing out to take the requisite picture of their kids surrounded by bluebonnets – Texas' state flower. From March to April in the Hill Country, orange Indian paintbrushes, deep-purple wine-cups and white-to-blue bluebonnets are at their peak.

If a visit to the Lady Bird Johnson Wildflower Center (p70) in South Austin has you itching for more blooms, hit the road for the nearby Hill County. To see vast cultivated fields of color, there's **Wildseed Farms** (☎830-990-1393; www.wildseedfarms.com; 100 Legacy Dr; admission free; ◷9:30am-6pm), which is 7 miles east of Fredericksburg on Hwy 290.

For a more do-it-yourself experience, check with the Texas Department of Transportation (TXDOT) **Wildflower Hotline** (☎800-452-9292) to find out what's blooming where. Taking Rte 16 and FM 1323, north from Fredericksburg and east to Willow City, is usually a good route. Then again you might just set to wandering – most back roads host their own shows daily. At visitor centers, look for the *Texas Wildflowers* pamphlet from *Texas Highways* magazine. It identifies Lone Star flowers and provides routes for scenic wildflower drives.

Mozart's Coffee Roasters

COFFEE

14 ☎ MAP P118, B1

Out on Lake Austin, you'll find a great waterfront view and a sinful dessert case. (☎512-477-2900; 3825 Lake Austin Blvd; ◷7am-midnight Mon-Thu, 7am-1am Fri, 8am-1am Sat, 8am-midnight Sun)

Shopping

Barton Creek Mall

MALL

15 🔒 MAP P118, E8

This indoor mall in southwest Austin has your standard mall offerings. (☎512-327-7041; www.simon.com/mall/barton-creek-square; 2901 S Capital of Texas Hwy; ◷10am-9pm Mon-Sat, 11am-7pm Sun)

West Austin

Bluebonnet and Indian paintbrush wildflowers

Walking Tour 🥾

Dripping Springs: Small Town Exploring

A small historic district sits along Mercer St in the center of sprawling Dripping Springs, a rural bedroom community about 25 miles west of Austin. The area is known for its outdoor attractions as well as its wineries, crafts breweries and distilleries, but if you don't feel like driving, downtown is an easy and welcoming place to explore by foot, and is especially fun from late afternoon into evening.

Walk Facts

Start Mazama Coffee Co

End Mercer Street Dance Hall

End 0.5 miles; 20 minutes

Getting there About 30 minutes by car from downtown Austin via Hwy 290

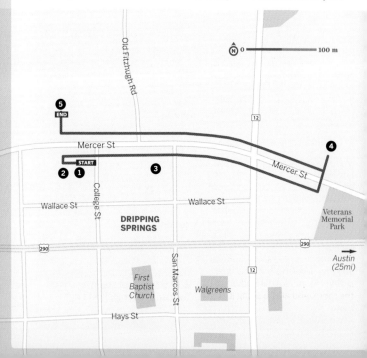

❶ Coffee with a Smile

You won't find snobby baristas at the ranch-style **Mazama Coffee Co** (📞512-200-6472; www.mazama coffee.com; 301 Mercer St; ⏰6:30am-6pm Mon-Fri, 8am-5pm Sat, 8am-1pm Sun; 📶) in the morning, just on-the-ball employees who manage to chitchat while keeping the long line moving efficiently. Be sure to order a breakfast taco – if there are any left. In the afternoon, the sunny patio is a nice place to read, meet a friend or work on your laptop while sipping the house-roasted coffee.

❷ Antiques & Indie Shops

A few doors down, step into **Lone Star Gifts** (📞512-858-9912; www. lonestargifts.net; 301 Mercer St) for an eclectic array of antiques and collectibles from more than 60 vendors. For essential oils, teas and organic herbs visit **Sacred Moon Herbs** (305 Mercer St; www. sacredmoonherbs.com) next door.

❸ No Haircuts Here

Every country town needs at least one hipster bar filled with millennials...right? We jest, but you'll likely spot several microbrew-sipping twentysomethings in the **Barber Shop** (📞512-829-4636; www.barber shopbar.com; 207 Mercer St; ⏰3-11pm Mon-Sat, 2-8pm Sun). If you squint you might just see some Gen-Xers and maybe even a baby boomer sitting around the dark edges of the room. And all are doing just fine at this one-time barber shop. The building, which also did time as a garage, dates to 1924.

❹ Eating at a Friend's House

There's something about **Homespun** (📞512-829-4064; www. homespunkitchenandbar.com; 131 E Mercer St; lunch mains $12-17, dinner mains $17-45; ⏰11am-9pm Tue-Thu, to 10pm Fri & Sat, 10am-8pm Sun) that makes you feel like you're chowing down at the cozy home of a good friend – one who also happens to be a fantastic Southern cook. How cozy? You might bump against the band on the front patio as you walk inside. The dining room is a festive place where the chatty owner might just tell you what's tasting good that evening. What's always good? The comfort food mainstays like shrimp and grits, burgers and skillet mac-n-cheese.

❺ Dance On

A bad mood dissolves the moment you step into **Mercer Street Dance Hall** (📞512-858-4314; www. mercerstreetdancehall.com; 332 Mercer St; tickets $7-15, free on Thu; ⏰6-11pm Thu, 7pm-midnight Fri, 7pm-1am Sat), where skilled dancers, ice cold beers and a welcoming communal spirit are always on the line-up. Open since 2013, this is one of the region's newest dance halls, but it's embraced the traditions of the classic Texas dance halls in full force, with dance lessons on Saturday nights and top regional acts performing on stage. There are no rules, but standing still on the dance floor just ain't right.

Explore
San Antonio

Much the most attractive of Texas' major cities — and much the oldest, too, having celebrated its 300th birthday in 2018 — San Antonio continues to delight visitors. The legendary Alamo, symbol of Texan independence, stands at the very heart of the city, while the River Walk, a glorious network of waterside pathways that's tucked below street level and lined with bars and restaurants, offers leisurely strolling through downtown and beyond.

The Short List

○ **The Alamo (p130)** *Exploring the Shrine and the grounds of the famous fort.*

○ **River Walk (p132)** *Enjoying lunch by the San Antonio River, then hopping on a river taxi.*

○ **Pearl District (p142)** *Wandering through the farmers market on a Saturday morning.*

○ **Friendly Spot Ice House (p141)** *Sipping a craft beer outside with locals on a Sunday afternoon.*

○ **Mission San José (p141)** *Time-traveling to the 1700s while walking the well-preserved mission grounds.*

Getting There & Around

🚗 Downtown San Antonio is bordered by I-35, I-10 and I-37, with concentric rings of highways around the center. The I-35 connects with Austin.

🚌 Greyhound has a terminal downtown, while Megabus, which picks up and drops off 3 miles south of downtown, connects to Houston, Austin and Dallas–Fort Worth.

San Antonio's public-transport network, VIA Metropolitan Transit, operates numerous local bus routes. Passes, schedules and route maps are available at VIA's downtown information center.

San Antonio Map on p134

River Walk (p132) F11PHOTO/SHUTTERSTOCK ©

Top Experience 📷

Explore Texas' Historic Icon: The Alamo

It would be a shame to visit Austin without making the trip to San Antonio, home of the Alamo. Find out why the story of the Alamo can rouse a Texan's sense of state pride like few other things. For many, it's not so much a tourist attraction as a pilgrimage – you might notice some visitors getting downright dewy-eyed at the description of how a few hundred revolutionaries died defending the fort against thousands of Mexican troops.

◉ MAP P134, D5

📞 210-225-1391

www.thealamo.org

300 Alamo Plaza

admission free

🕑 by reservation 9am-5:30pm Sep-May, to 9pm Jun-Aug

The Building

The main chapel building is now known as the **Shrine**. From here you can set off for a free history talk in the Cavalry Courtyard, hearing one of many perspectives on the actual events – which are somewhat in dispute – or browse the museum in the Long Barrack, which served as a residence for the Spanish priests and later as a hospital for Mexican and Texan troops. There's also a 17-minute film, which not only gives you another perspective on the battle, but is an excellent place to escape the heat.

Walk the Alamo

If you're interested in walking the front perimeter of the old fort, which extends beyond the chapel, and learning more details about the battle and its participants, join the one-hour guided Battlefield Tour ($15 per person). A 33-stop audio tour ($7) is self-guided and takes about 45 minutes. (Visitors taking the guided tour are also given the audio tour, since the Battlefield Tour does not cover all 33 stops.)

A Series of Missions

The Alamo is the first (and most impressive) in a series of Spanish-constructed missions. With the destruction by war or disease of many East Texas missions, the Spanish quickly built four more missions south of the Alamo, now collectively known as the Mission Trail. Religious services are still held in these mission churches.

★ Top Tips

o Seeing the Alamo for the first time? Many people are surprised to see that it's in the middle of downtown San Antonio, surrounded by tacky tourist attractions. But even more startling is its diminutive size. Whether it's because of the monument's sentimental stature or too many tightly cropped photographs that don't offer any indication of scale, the first thing many people say when they first see the Alamo is, 'Wow, it's a lot smaller than I thought it would be!'

✕ Take a Break

Founded in 1917, nearby **Schilo's German Delicatessen** (☎210-223-6692; www.schilos.com; 424 E Commerce St; mains breakfast $6-8, lunch & dinner $6-9; ☉7am-8:30pm Mon-Sat) offers good-value breakfasts and lunches.

Top Experience 📷

Stroll along San Antonio's River Walk

A little slice of Europe in the heart of downtown San Antonio, the 15-mile River Walk is an essential part of the San Antonio experience. This is no ordinary riverfront, but a charming canal and pedestrian street that is the main artery at the heart of the city's tourism efforts.

◎ MAP P134, D6

www.thesanantonio
riverwalk.com

Background

In 1921 floods destroyed downtown San Antonio when water 10ft deep gushed through the center of the city from the overflowing San Antonio River. As a result, the Olmos Dam was constructed to handle overflow and route the extra water around the downtown area through a canal called the Oxbow.

In 1938 the Works Progress Administration (WPA) assumed control of the canal's fate, and executed a plan to develop a central business district of shops and restaurants along a cobbled walk. More than 1000 jobs were created during the construction of the River Walk, and the project is one of the most beautiful results of the WPA effort.

Riverfront Activities

You can meander past landscaped hotel gardens and riverside cafes, and linger on the stone footbridges that stretch over the water. During summer it gets mighty crowded, but at peaceful times (and as you get away from downtown) it's a lovely place to stroll, especially during the holidays, when it's bedecked with twinkling lights.

Feeling athletic? Once out of downtown, cycling to San Antonio's missions or museums via the River Walk is also an option. Check with **B-cycle** (☏210-281-0101; https://sanantonio. bcycle.com; day/monthly pass $12/18), San Antonio's bicycle-sharing scheme, for rental locations.

River Walk Extension

The River Walk used to be just a downtown thing, but a $358-million project completed in 2013 extended it to the north and south. As part of the 8-mile Mission Reach expansion, you can walk south to the King William District and beyond to the Spanish missions. The 4-mile Museum Reach stretches north to the San Antonio Museum of Art (p142), the Pearl Brewery complex (p142) and Brackenridge Park (p136).

★ Top Tips

○ For the best River Walk overview, hop on a Go Rio San Antonio river cruise (p137).

✗ Take a Break

Dining and drinking options abound along the River Walk. Cool off with a house-made Italian-style ice cream from **Justin's Ice Cream Company** (☏210-222-2707; 245 E Commerce St; small/ large serving $4/6; ⊙11am-11pm) on the riverfront.

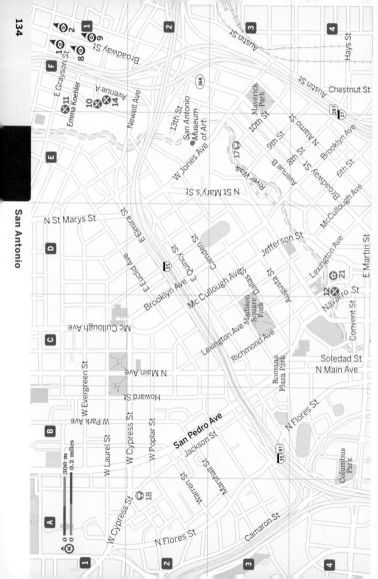

San Antonio

N Cherry St

Nolan St

Healy
Murphy
Park

E Houston St

E Crockett St

Center St

Amtrak
Station

Hoefgen Ave

Montana St

Alamodome

N St Mary's St

Avenue E

E 4th St

San Antonio
Visitor Information
Center

The 3rd St
Alamo

Alamo Plaza

E Crockett St

Elm St

Bowie St

E Crockett St

E Commerce St

E Market St

Henry B González
Convention Center

Tower
of the
Americas

S Bowie St

E César E Chávez Blvd

Labor St

Jefferson St

Buckhorn
Saloon &
Museum

College St

River
Walk

E Commerce St

Go Rio

S Alamo St

Villita St

Hemisfair
Park

Lavaca St

Camargo St

Soledad St
N Main Ave

N Houston St

San
Fernando
Cathedral

Briscoe Western
Art Museum

San Antonio River

River Walk

Arciniega St

KING
WILLIAM
DISTRICT

S Presa St

S Alamo St

Turner St

Madison St

Beauregard St

Spanish
Governor's
Palace

Dolorosa St

Dwyer Ave

S Main Ave

S St Mary's St

E César E Chávez Blvd

Washington St

River Walk

E Arsenal St

W Houston St

Camaron St

Market
Square

Dolorosa St

S Flores St

W Nueva St

San Pedro Creek

Milam
Park

N San Saba

W Commerce St

Dolorosa St

S Santa Rosa Ave

W César E
Chávez Blvd

E Paso St

For reviews see
◆ Top Experiences   p130
◉ Sights   p136
✕ Eating   p139
🍷 Drinking   p141
✦ Entertainment   p142

Sights

McNay Art Museum MUSEUM

1 ⊙ MAP P134, F1

This Spanish Colonial revival-style mansion, 5 miles north of downtown and originally owned by Marion Koogler McNay, is spectacular. McNay's collection of European and American art, which she left to the city after her death in 1950, is even more stunning. Wandering from room to room, you encounter treasure after treasure, with Picasso's *Woman With a Plumed Hat* and Van Gogh's *Women Crossing the Fields* standing out amid works by Matisse, Cézanne, Munch, Rodin and more besides. (📞210-824-5368; www.mcnayart.org; 6000 N New Braunfels Ave; adult/child under

20yr $20/free, special exhibits extra; ⏰10am-6pm Wed & Fri, to 9pm Thu, to 5pm Sat, noon-5pm Sun, grounds 7am-7pm Mar-Oct, to 6pm Nov-Feb)

Brackenridge Park PARK

2 ⊙ MAP P134, F1

North of downtown near Trinity University, this 343-acre park is a great place to spend a family day. As well as the San Antonio Zoo (p139), you'll find the **Kiddie Park** (📞210-824-4351; www.kiddiepark.com; 3015 Broadway; 1 ticket $2.50, 6 tickets $11.25, day pass $13; ⏰10am-7pm Wed-Sun Mar-Aug, 10am-7pm Fri-Sun Sep-Feb; 👫), the **Japanese Tea Garden** (📞210-212-4814; www.saparksfoundation.org/japanese-tea-garden; 3853 N St Marys St; admission free; ⏰dawn-dusk), the San Antonio

McNay Art Museum

Zoo Eagle miniature train and an old-fashioned carousel. (www.brackenridgepark.org; 3700 N St Marys St; train $4, carousel $2.50; ⏰5am-11pm; 👨‍👩‍👧)

Go Rio
CRUISE

3 🎯 MAP P134, D6

These 35-minute narrated cruises leave every 15 to 20 minutes, and give a good visual overview of the river plus a light history lesson. No reservations are necessary; buy tickets online, at the ticket booth at 706 River Walk, or at any of the other boarding points listed on the website. (☎210-227-4746; www.goriocruises.com; 706 River Walk; tour $13.50, river taxi 24hr pass $19.50; ⏰9am-10pm)

San Fernando Cathedral
HISTORIC BUILDING

4 🎯 MAP P134, C6

Founded in 1731, San Antonio's cathedral ranks as the oldest church in Texas. Its prime interest for modern visitors is as the screen – literally – for *San Antonio: The Saga*. This after-dark sound-and-light show, telling the story of the city with dazzling colorful effects, is projected onto the facade on four nights weekly (9pm, 9:30pm and 10pm, Tuesday and Friday to Sunday; free; www.mainplaza.org). (☎210-227-1297; www.sfcathedral.org; 115 W Main Plaza; ⏰gift shop 9am-1pm & 2-5pm Mon-Sat, 8:30am-3:30pm Sun)

San Antonio in a Day

Start your day at the River Walk (p132), then take some time to remember the Alamo (p130). Check out whatever downtown sights you fancy, perhaps the Buckhorn Museum or the Briscoe Western Art Museum (p138). Later, explore the historic homes of the King William District and plan on dinner anywhere along Alamo St.

Buckhorn Saloon & Museum
MUSEUM

5 🎯 MAP P134, D5

Waaaay back in 1881, when the Buckhorn Saloon first opened, the owner promised patrons a free beer or shot for any deer antlers they brought in. Although the location has changed, you can still see the collection – and the bar – at today's Buckhorn Saloon, downtown. You don't need a ticket to sip an overpriced beverage in the saloon, beneath the collective gaze of a giraffe, a bear and all manner of mounted horned beasts. (☎210-247-4000; www.buckhornmuseum.com; 318 E Houston St; adult/child 3-11yr $23/17; ⏰10am-5pm Sun-Thu, to 6pm Fri & Sat, to 9pm daily mid-Jun–early Sep)

Explore San Antonio on Four Wheels

Cycle racks all around downtown, now branded as SWell Cycle (p133) but widely known by the former name of B-cycle, make hopping on a bike convenient and tempting. It's great for sightseeing beyond downtown; dock your bike at a station when you're done using it, and the meter stops. Come back when you're ready, hop on any bike and go.

You'll find stations at most major tourist destinations, from the Witte Museum in the north all the way south to the four missions. The River Walk is closed to cycling in the heart of downtown, but you can cycle along the river further out. Download the free B-cycle smartphone app for route details or ask about routes at the **visitor center** (Map p134, D5; ☎210-244-2000; www.visitsanantonio.com; 317 Alamo Plaza; ⊙9am-5pm).

A single ride costs $3, while a $12 day pass allows a day's worth of unlimited bike trips of up to 60 minutes each (there's a charge of $2 for every 30 minutes beyond that).

Spanish Governor's Palace
HISTORIC BUILDING

6 ◉ MAP P134, B6

The name now attached to this low-profile adobe structure is an exaggeration. When built in 1722, it was the home and office of the captain of the local presidio. Now restored to something close to its original appearance, and outfitted with period furnishings, it's a great place to learn about the early days of San Antonio. (☎210-224-0601; www.spanishgovernorspalace.org; 105 Plaza de Armas; adult/child 7-13yr $5/3; ⊙9am-5pm Tue-Sat, 10am-5pm Sun)

Briscoe Western Art Museum
MUSEUM

7 ◉ MAP P134, D6

Devoted as much to general Western history as it is to art, this small downtown museum pays its respects to cowboys, Hispanic settlers, Native Americans and the women of the west. Along with weaponry, uniforms, 1880s' photographs of Yosemite National Park, a saddle that belonged to Pancho Villa, and recordings of Western songs, you'll find all sorts of landscapes and portraits, plus a large and fascinating diorama that depicts the fall of the Alamo. (☎210-299-4499; www.briscoemuseum.org; 210 W Market St; adult/child under 13yr $10/free; ⊙10am-5pm Mon & Wed-Sat, to 9pm Tue, to 3pm Sun)

Witte Museum
MUSEUM

8 ⊙ MAP P134, F1

Set on the eastern edge of
Brackenridge Park, the Witte is
an engaging museum of natural
history, science and Texas history.
Pronounced 'witty', it's targeted
especially at local schoolkids, with
hands-on exhibitions covering top-
ics like dinosaurs, the Peoples of
the Pecos, and regional wildlife. A
model of the winged *Quetzalcoat-
lus*, the largest flying creature ever
to exist, hangs above the foyer.
(📞210-357-1900; www.wittemu-
seum.org; 3801 Broadway St; adult/
child 4-11yr $14/10, 3-8pm Tue free;
🕐10am-5pm Mon & Wed-Sat, to 8pm
Tue, noon-5pm Sun; 👫)

San Antonio Zoo
ZOO

9 ⊙ MAP P134, F1

San Antonio's zoo, in Brecken-
ridge Park north of downtown,
is home to 9000 animals from
750 different species. As well
as one of the country's largest
endangered-animal collections, it
features a mini-train, a carousel
and a butterfly garden. All charge a
small separate fee, or are included
in the Fun Day ticket (adult/child
$25/22), which offers a small
overall saving. (📞210-734-7184;
www.sazoo.org; 3903 N St Marys St;
adult/child $16.90/13.35; 🕐9am-5pm
Mon-Fri, to 6pm Sat & Sun, to 8pm Sat
& Sun Jun-Aug; 👫)

Eating

Bakery Lorraine
CAFE $

10 🍴 MAP P134, F1

There's a reason why everyone you
see in the Pearl District seems to
be carrying a box from Bakery Lorraine – the pastries are delicious.
Macaroons. Tarts. Cookies. You
won't walk away empty-handed.
And with plentiful seating in the
bright interior, and patio tables
perfect for a spring day, it's also a
great spot for a gourmet lunchtime
sandwich or salad. (📞210-862-
5582; www.bakerylorraine.com; 306
Pearl Pkwy; pastries $3-6, salads &
sandwiches $7-10; 🕐7am-8pm)

Green Vegetarian Cuisine
VEGETARIAN $

11 🍴 MAP P134, F1

San Antonio's pioneer vegetarian restaurant has an appealing
location in the Pearl Brewery
complex, with lots of outdoor seating. Not only are dishes like the
portabella burger, the 'Big Nasty'
chickpea burger, the 'fishless' fish
and chips, and the enchiladas all
100% vegetarian, they're also
100% kosher, and any meal can be
made vegan. (📞210-320-5865; www.
eatatgreen.com; 200 E Grayson St;
mains breakfast $4-8, lunch & dinner
$8-12; 🕐8am-9pm Mon-Thu, to 8pm
Fri, 9am-9pm Sun, closed Sat; 🍴)

Ocho at
Hotel Havana

CUBAN $$

12 MAP P134, D4

Set in a tall, narrow glassed-in conservatory, perched above the quiet northern stretch of the River Walk, this hotel restaurant makes a pleasant 20-minute stroll from downtown on a warm evening. Its Cuban-inspired menu is relatively short, but mains like the bone-in pork chop with chorizo Brussels sprouts are excellent, and you can get everything from breakfast to late-night cocktails. (210-222-2008; www.havanasanantonio.com; 1015 Navarro St; mains breakfast $12-16, lunch & dinner $12-28; 7am-10pm Sun-Thu, to midnight Fri & Sat;)

Mi Tierra
Cafe & Bakery

TEX-MEX $$

13 MAP P134, B6

Part restaurant, part bakery, and total explosion of light and color, decorated for Christmas year-round, this Market Sq behemoth has been dishing out Mexican staples since 1941. Its interlinked dining rooms are busy with scuttling waitstaff and strolling mariachis, and there's always a long line for takeout pastries and pies. Open 24 hours, it's ideal for 3am enchilada cravings. (210-225-1262; www.mitierracafe.com; Market Sq, 218 Produce Row; mains $9-29; 24hr)

Cured

AMERICAN $$$

14 MAP P134, F1

Mighty slabs of meat hang smack-dab in the center of the dining room at this Pearl District crowd-pleaser, where charcuterie platters ($20 to $36) are loaded with meats, spreads, pickles and crackers. At lunch, look for daily gourmet po'boys and a few salads and sandwiches. Dinner is a carnivore's delight, with pork cheeks, roasted bone marrow, spiced quail and more. (210-314-3929; www.curedatpearl.com; 306 Pearl Pkwy; mains lunch $12-28, dinner $20-42; 11am-3pm & 5-11pm Mon-Fri, 10am-3pm & 5-11pm Sat)

Las Canarias

NEW AMERICAN $$$

15 MAP P134, C5

American standards are classed up with a dash of global flair at the signature restaurant in the upscale Omni La Mansion del Rio hotel. Shrimp and grits with chorizo, anyone? The River Walk patio makes a more romantic setting than the indoor room. (210-518-1063; www.omnihotels.com; 112 College St; mains breakfast $11-19, lunch $12-21, dinner $27-49; 6:30am-10pm Mon-Thu, to 11pm Fri & Sat, 10am-10pm Sun)

Drinking

Friendly Spot Ice House   BAR

16 MAP P134, C8

This place feels like a big neighborhood party where everyone is getting along. What could be more inviting than a pecan-tree-shaded yard filled with colorful lawn chairs? Friends (and their dogs) gather to knock back longnecks –

as well as 300 bottled beers, there are 76 on tap – while the kids amuse themselves in the playground area. (210-224-2337; www.thefriendlyspot.com; 943 S Alamo St; noon-midnight;)

VFW Post 76   BAR

17 MAP P134, E3

We're giving this hidden-away joint, on the River Walk near the

San Antonio's Mission Trail

Spain's missionary presence can best be felt at the ruins of the four missions south of town, all overseen by the National Park Service as part of the **San Antonio Missions National Historical Park** (www.nps.gov/saan; admission free). The main park visitor center is at **Mission San José** (210-932-1001; 6701 San José Dr; 9am-5pm), which is the best place to start before exploring the missions. You'll find helpful trip-planning information on the park website.

The San Antonio missions were constructed in the early 18th century as part of an effort to provide way-stations and staging areas for Spanish colonial expansion to the north. The native Coahuiltecans, already under pressure from other nomadic Native American tribes pushing down from the north, showed a willingness to convert to Christianity, and labored for the colonial Spanish priests in order to receive food and protection at the missions.

Constructed in what is now downtown, the first and most impressive mission was what would come to be known as the Alamo (p130). With the destruction by war or disease of many East Texas missions, the Spanish quickly built four more missions south of the Alamo, now collectively known as the Mission Trail. Religious services are still held in the mission churches.

The **Mission Reach**, an 8-mile extension of the River Walk (p132), connects downtown with all four missions. South of the Blue Star Arts Complex, the River Walk becomes a pretty walking and cycling trail, open from dawn to dusk.

Pearl development, a medal for outstanding service as a dive bar. But don't get us wrong – it's one of the classiest dives you'll ever visit, where hipsters and old-timers chug longnecks side by side in a two-story Victorian house that's the oldest Veterans of Foreign Wars post in Texas. (📞210-223-4581; www.vfwpost76ontheriverwalk.org; 10 10th St; 🕑noon-midnight Mon-Thu, to 2am Fri-Sun)

The Cove
BEER HALL

18 🍺 MAP P134, A2

Live music is just part of the reason to hang out at this chill beer hall, which has more than 50 Texas beers on tap. The Cove is a unique combo of food-stand/cafe/laundromat/car-wash – it even has a kiddie playground. The restaurant (tacos $4 to $5, burgers $9 to $13) closes one hour earlier than the bar Tuesday through Saturday. (📞210-227-2683; www.thecove.us; 606 W Cypress St; 🕑11am-11pm Tue-Thu & Sun, to midnight Fri & Sat; 👫)

Entertainment

Magik Children's Theatre
THEATER

19 ⭐ MAP P134, D7

This merry troupe stages adaptations of favorite children's books, hilarious original musicals and modern retellings of Texas legends and classic fairy tales, such as the witty, bilingual *La Cinderella*. Check the website for details of contemporary plays for adults, plus summertime Shakespeare performances along the River Walk. (📞210-227-2751; www.magiktheatre.org; 420 S Alamo St; $15; 🕑box office 9am-5pm Mon-Fri, noon-4pm Sat & Sun; 👫)

A City Built on Beer

San Antonio was once a brewing town, home to two of Texas' largest breweries: the Lone Star Brewery and Pearl Brewery were both established by German settlers in the late 1800s. And while both of them eventually shut down, they left behind two remarkable buildings.

The Lone Star Brewery has provided an impressive setting for the **San Antonio Museum of Art** (Map p134, E2; SAMA; www.samuseum.org; 200 W Jones Ave; adult/child under 12yr $20/free; 🕑10am-5pm Wed, Thu, Sat & Sun, to 7pm Tue & Fri), which opened in 1981. And the old Pearl Brewery has received a massive face-lift as part of the new **Pearl District** (www.atpearl.com; 200 E Grayson St) development north of downtown, including shops, cafes and restaurants. Looks like beer wasn't the only good thing to come out of these breweries.

Mission San José (p141)

Majestic Theatre
THEATER

20 ⭐ MAP P134, C5

Head to historic, city-owned Majestic Theatre downtown for its program of musical concerts, touring Broadway shows and numerous other live events at any time of year. (📞210-226-5700, box office 210-226-3333; www.majesticempire.com; 224 E Houston St; ⏱box office 10am-5pm Mon-Fri, hours vary Sat)

Tobin Center for the Performing Arts
THEATER

21 ⭐ MAP P134, D4

On the River Walk, San Antonio's performance hall hosts performances by Ballet San Antonio and the San Antonio Symphony. The innovative in-house theater company **Attic Rep** (www.atticrep.org) produces shows that are edgy, compelling and current. (📞210-223-8624; www.tobincenter.org; 100 Auditorium Circle; ⏱box office 10am-6pm Mon-Fri, to 2pm Sat, plus 1hr before showtime)

Survival Guide

Electric-vehicle charging point ROSCHETZKY PHOTOGRAPHY/SHUTTERSTOCK ©

Before You Go

Book Your Stay

o There's no shortage of rooms, until major events come to town, such as SXSW, the Formula 1 Grand Prix, the Austin City Limits Festival and the Thanksgiving Day football game between UT and Texas A&M.

o At these times prices skyrocket and rooms are booked months in advance. At other times, choose accommodations as close to downtown as you can afford.

o Chains border I-35, and while they may not offer the best Austin experience, great deals can be found.

Useful Websites

Lonely Planet (www. lonelyplanet.com/usa/ austin/hotels) Reviews of Lonely Planet's top choices.

Visit Austin (www. austintexas.org/ visit/stay/hotels) City tourism website with

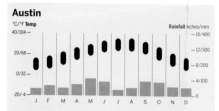

Austin

When to Go

o **Spring (Mar–May)** Wildflowers and mild weather make this the perfect time of year to visit. Temperatures get hot in May.

o **Summer (Jun–Aug)** The weather is hot but bearable, and everything is still green for the most part.

o **Fall (Sep–Nov)** You won't see any fall foliage, but temperatures will have cooled by now.

o **Winter (Dec–Feb)** Temperatures can drop below 40° F, but warm and mild conditions are the norm. Snow is rare.

overview of accommodation options plus lodging summaries.

Best Budget

Best Western Plus – Austin City (www. bestwestern.com) Complimentary breakfast is the bomb.

Firehouse Hostel (www.firehousehostel. com) Downtown hostel with a pub.

City View Inn & Suites at Sunset Station (www.cityviewinns.

com) Clean and modern with shared amenities and free parking in San Antonio.

Best Inns & Small Hotels

Heywood Hotel (www. heywoodhotel.com) Style and hospitality in East Austin.

Kimber Modern (www.kimbermodern. com) A posh and tranquil oasis near S Congress Ave.

Hill Country Casitas
(www.hillcountry casitas.com) Stone cottages on a terraced hillside.

Hotel Ella (www.hotel-ella.com) History and art near the University of Texas.

Best Boutique Hotels

Hotel Van Zandt (www. hotelvanzandt.com) Glossy, music-themed and overlooking the lake.

South Congress Hotel (www.southcongress hotel.com) Great patios and bars for people-watching.

Hotel San José (www. sanjosehotel.com) Stylish courtyard is the place to be.

Hotel St Cecilia (www. hotelsaintcecilia.com) As exclusive as you can get in Austin.

Lone Star Court (www.lonestarcourt. com) Cowboy cool with loads of amenities.

Hotel Emma (www. thehotelemma.com) Steampunk-glam in San Antonio's Pearl District.

Arriving in Austin

Austin-Bergstrom International Airport

Opened in 1999, Austin-Bergstrom International Airport is about 10 miles south-east of downtown. It's served by Air Canada, Alaska Airlines, Allegiant, American, British Airways, Delta, Frontier, JetBlue, Southwest, United and Virgin America.

Taxi Between the airport and downtown costs $25 to $30.

Capital Metro
(CapMetro; ☎ 512-474-1200; www.capmetro.org) Runs a limited-stop service (bus 20) between the airport and downtown and the University of Texas for just $1.25 each way, with departures every 15 minutes. Check website for exact schedules. It takes at least 20 minutes to get downtown

from the airport, and 35 minutes to reach the UT campus.

SuperShuttle
(☎ 800-258-3826; www. supershuttle.com) Offers a shared-van service from the airport to downtown hotels for about $14 one way, or a few dollars more to accommodations along N I-35 and near the Arboretum Mall.

Rental Cars Walk from the terminal to the rental car facility. All major rental car agencies are represented.

Rideshare Companies that pick-up and drop-off passengers at the airport include Fare (www.ridefare. com), Fasten (www. fasten.com) and the nonprofit Ride Austin (www.rideaustin.com), plus a few others. Uber (www.uber.com) and Lyft (www.lyft.com) operate in the city.

Bus

Greyhound (☎ 512-458-4463; www.grey hound.com; 916 E Koenig Lane) The Greyhound station is 5 miles north of downtown. Capital Metro bus 10-South

Arriving in San Antonio

The Alamo and the River Walk are smack dab in the middle of downtown. It's well worth venturing further afield, though, to such highlights as the McNay Art Museum, the revitalized Pearl District nearby, and the charming King William neighborhood south of downtown.

San Antonio International Airport

The **airport** (SAT; ☎ 210-207-3433; www.sanantonio.gov/sat; 9800 Airport Blvd) is 8 miles north of downtown, just north of the intersection of Loop 410 and US 281. Frequent flights connect it with destinations in Texas, the rest of the USA, and Mexico. Terminal A is used by AeroMexico, Alaska Airlines, Delta, Frontier, Interjet, Southwest, US Airways and Volaris, while Terminal B houses American and United Airlines.

VIA (☎ 210-362-2020; www.viainfo.net) bus 5 runs at least hourly between the airport and downtown from around 5:30am (6am on weekends) until 9:30pm or so. The regular service costs $1.30; the journey takes about 40 minutes. The VIA stop is on the Lower Roadway at Arrivals/Baggage Claim. Walk to the outer curb; the stop is at the far west end of Terminal B.

The airport is served by taxis, public transportation, shuttles and Uber, Lyft and GetMe. A taxi ride from the airport to downtown costs from $29 for up to four people. Major downtown hotels have free airport courtesy shuttles; be sure to ask when booking.

Bus

Greyhound (☎ 210-270-5868; www.greyhound.com; 500 N St Marys St) has a terminal downtown, while **Megabus** (☎ 877-462-6342; www.usmegabus.com; 840 Probandt St), which picks up and drops off 3 miles south of downtown, connects to Houston, Austin and Dallas–Fort Worth.

Car & Motorcycle

Downtown San Antonio is bordered by I-35, I-10 and I-37, with concentric rings of highways around the center. I-35 connects Austin and San Antonio, and I-10 connects San Antonio with Houston to the east and El Paso to the west. For information on parking in San Antonio, see p150.

All major rental-car agencies have outlets at San Antonio International Airport, and some have outlets downtown as well.

Train

Squeezed between Sunset Station and the Alamodome, the **Amtrak station** (☎ 800-872-7245; www.amtrak.com; 350 Hoefgen Ave) is served by the Sunset Limited and Texas Eagle train services.

First/Red River (www.capmetro.org) will deliver you from the station to downtown. Buses leave from here for other major Texas cities frequently.

Megabus (www.megabus.com; 1500 San Jacinto Blvd) Pick-up and drop-off stop at 1500 San Jacinto Blvd on the northeast corner of the state capitol grounds.

Train

Amtrak (www.amtrak.com; 250 N Lamar Blvd) The downtown station is served by the Texas Eagle, which extends from Chicago to Los Angeles. There's free parking and an enclosed waiting area but no staff. Fares vary wildly.

Getting Around Austin

Bicycle

A grand bicycle tour of greater Austin isn't feasible, due to interstate highways and the like, but cycling around downtown, South Congress and the UT campus is totally doable. There are also miles of recreational paths around the city that are ideal for cruisin'. Check www.austintexas.gov/bicycle for a route map. You'll also find routes and maps at www.bicycleaustin.info.

The city also offers bike sharing, with more than 40 **Austin B-cycle** (www.austin.bcycle.com) stations scattered around the city.

Say what you will about Lance Armstrong, you can still count on him to find you a pretty good bike. Located right downtown, **Mellow Johnny's Bike Shop** (Map p40; ☎512-473-0222; www.mellowjohnnys.com; 400 Nueces St; day use $20-50; ☺7am-7pm Mon-Fri, 7am-6pm Sat, 8am-5pm Sun) is co-owned by the disgraced seven-time Tour de France winner. It rents high-performance bikes as well as commuter bikes, and offers free guided bike rides (check the website for a schedule).

Looking for something a little more casual? The cool thing about **Bicycle Sport Shop** (Map p74; ☎512-477-3472; www.bicyclesportshop.com; 517 S Lamar Blvd; per 2hr from $16; ☺10am-7pm Mon-Fri, 9am-6pm Sat, 11am-5pm Sun) is its proximity to Zilker Park, Barton Springs and the Lady Bird Lake bike paths, all of which are within a few blocks. Rentals range from $16 for a two-hour cruise on a standard bike to $60 for a full day on a top-end full-suspension model. On weekends and holidays, advance reservations are advised.

Car & Motorcycle

Getting around Austin is easy enough, but the main consideration for drivers – other than rush-hour gridlock and what people from other towns consider crazy drivers – is where to leave your car when you're not in it.

Downtown, the best deal is at the **Capitol Visitors Parking Garage** (1201 San Jacinto Blvd). It's free for the first two hours, and only $1 per half-hour after that, maxing out at $12. Other downtown garages and lots are fairly abundant. They usually charge $2 to $3 per hour, with a daily maximum of $10 to $18.

Other downtown garages and parking lots typically charge a flat fee of around $7 to $10 or so after dark. People also park for free under I-35 at the east end of 6th St, but you can't depend on it being available (or legal).

Parking meters downtown cost $1.20 per hour. Outside of downtown they usually run about $1 per hour, although rates may vary on the UT campus or within the State Capitol Complex. Gone are the days of free downtown street parking on nights and weekends. However, to discourage drunk driving after partying downtown, the city implemented the Get Home Safe Program. You can now prepay at meters that have yellow Next Day buttons. If you forget to prepay, you may have the ticket waived if you complete and email a waiver form stating you took a safe ride home. Your car will not be towed – unless you park on 6th St between Red River and Brazos Sts. Visit www.austintexas.gov/gethomesafe for more overnight parking and safe travel options.

Elsewhere around Austin, you can find free on-street parking, but pay careful attention to posted permit parking and time limits.

Day or night, finding a spot around the UT campus can take a while. Free visitor parking is available outside the LBJ Library in Lot 38, but from there it's a long, hot walk across campus to the UT Tower and other sights. Parking spots on Guadalupe St are both timed and metered. Otherwise, your best bet is to search for free parking in the residential streets west of Guadalupe St.

Public Transportation

Austin's handy public-transit system is run

Parking in San Antonio

When visiting downtown, you'll definitely want to ditch your car, but street parking is hard to find. There are plenty of public parking lots downtown, including with most of the major hotels; the lots generally cost $3 per hour, or $5 to $10 for 24 hours. Here are some alternatives:

o Park on the street for free in the residential King William District or Southtown, then take the 11 VIA bus (dubbed 'the Culture Route').

o Park for free at **VIA Ellis Alley Park & Ride** (212 Chestnut St, btwn E Crockett & Center Sts) then pay $2.60 round-trip to ride downtown.

o Park inexpensively at **Market Square** (612 W Commerce St; parking flat rate $10-11), then walk 15 minutes to the Alamo.

o Park at **Riverbend Garage** (210 N Presa; daily parking $2-16; ⊙24hr), which is a little more expensive but puts you right in the heart of things.

by **Capital Metro** (CapMetro; ☎512-474-1200; www.capmetro.org). Call for directions to anywhere or stop in at the downtown **Capital Metro Transit Store** (☎512-389-7454; 209 W 9th St; ⏱7:30am-5:30pm Mon-Fri) for information. Regular city buses – not including the more expensive express routes – cost $1.25. Children under six years of age are free. Almost all CapMetro buses, including more than a dozen UT shuttle routes, have bicycle racks on front, to which you can hitch your bike for free.

Rideshare

For ridesharing, try Fare (www.ridefare.com), Fasten (www.fasten.com) or the nonprofit Ride Austin (www.rideaustin.com). Uber (www.uber/com) and Lyft (www.lyft.com) operate in the city.

Taxi

You'll usually need to call for a cab instead of just flagging one down on the street, except at the airport, at major hotels, around the state capitol and at major entertainment areas. The flag drops at $2.50, then it's $2.40 for each additional mile. Larger companies include **Yellow Cab** (☎512-452-9999) and **Austin Cab** (☎512-478-2222).

Human-powered bicycle taxis (pedicabs) are available downtown on 6th St and around the Warehouse District, usually from about 9pm until after 2am from Wednesday to Saturday evenings. The drivers, who are typically young students or musicians, work entirely for tips, so please be generous.

Essential Information

Accessible Travel

Download Lonely Planet's free Accessible Travel guide from https://shop.lonelyplanet.com/categories/accessible-travel.

Public Spaces

○ **Guide dogs** May legally be brought into restaurants, hotels and other businesses.

○ **Lodging** Most hotels and motels have rooms set aside for disabled guests.

○ **Public buildings** Hotels, restaurants, theaters, museums etc are required by the Americans with Disabilities Act (ADA) to be wheelchair accessible and have accessible restroom facilities.

○ **Road crossings** Street crossings are dangerous in Austin, with dozens of fatalities over the years. City Council has been considering audible crossing signals, but they are not yet in use.

Resources

Access-able Travel Source (www.access-able.com) Travel information and links.

Mobility International USA (www.miusa.org) Advises disabled travelers.

Wheelchair Getaways (www.accessible-minivans.com/texas-austin.htm) Van rental.

Business Hours

Individual opening hours are included in reviews; the following are generalities. Sight and activity hours vary and may decrease during the shoulder and low seasons.

Banks 9am to 5pm Monday to Friday

Restaurants 11am to 2pm and 5pm to 10pm, often without breaks.

Cafes 7am to 8pm

Nightclubs 8pm to 2am

Shops 9am to 6pm Monday to Saturday, 11am to 6pm Sunday

COVID-19

At time of writing, there are no COVID-related travel restrictions – apart from the requirement for non-US citizens to be fully vaccinated before entering the country. Most businesses in Austin are operating as normal, though some sites may keep shorter hours or require mask-wearing before entering.

Discount Cards

AAA Membership in the American Automobile Association (AAA) provides access to hotel room discounts, and some reduced admission as well as roadside assistance.

Seniors If you are over the age of 65, discount rates on hotel rooms and attractions may be available. Having an American Association of Retired Persons (AARP) card is not usually required.

Students An International Student Identity Card (ISIC) or official school ID card often gets you discounts on admission to museums and other attractions.

Electricity

Type A
120V/60Hz

Money

○ Credit cards are widely accepted, and they are generally required for reservations and car rentals.

○ ATMs accepting most network and credit cards are easily found, except in the most popular nightlife areas, where privately owned ATMs (look for them inside convenience stores or often right on the street) charge exorbitant transaction fees.

○ Bank of America exchanges foreign currency and traveler's checks. There is an exchange service at the airport, too.

Public Holidays

Banks, schools, and government offices (including post offices) are closed on major holidays. Public holidays that fall on a weekend are often observed on the following Monday.

New Year's Day January 1

Confederate Heroes' Day January 19

Martin Luther King Jr Day Third Monday in January

President's Day Third Monday in February

Texas Independence Day March 2

Easter Sunday March/April

Memorial Day Last Monday in May

Juneteenth June 19

Independence Day July 4

Labor Day First Monday in September

Columbus Day Second Monday in October

Veterans Day November 11

Thanksgiving Fourth Thursday in November

Christmas Day December 25

Safe Travel

○ Some folks may tell you that anywhere east of I-35 is dangerous. While there may be some truth to that, overt or covert racism may exaggerate such claims – this is a predominantly African American and Latino part of town.

○ One frequent complaint centers on drunken college students letting it all hang out on 6th St. It's a party atmosphere, and if you're drunkenly counting your cash and appraising your jewelry in an alley at 2am, you're likely to encounter interest.

○ There are often panhandlers downtown near Congress Ave, especially between 4th and 7th Sts. Keep your wits about you if you're returning to your car at night, or hail a taxi (or a pedicab).

○ Austin natives claim they live in the allergy capital of America, and at any time of year residents and visitors are likely to sneeze and wheeze. If you're at all susceptible, especially to pollen or mold, bring proper medication.

○ Take advantage of cooler mornings and evenings to do your exploring. During the high heat of midday, find a cool spot to unwind, like Barton Springs pool (p69).

Tourist Information

Austin Visitor Center

(512-478-0098; www. austintexas.org; 602 E 4th St; 9am-5pm Mon-Sat, from 10am Sun) Maps, brochures and gift shop downtown.

Capitol Visitors Center

(CVC; 512-305-8400; www.tspb. texas.gov/prop/tcvc/ cvc/cvc.html; 112 E 11th St; 9am-5pm Mon-Sat, noon-5pm Sun) Self-guided-tour booklets for the capitol itself, plus information and maps for Austin and the entire state.

San Antonio Visitor Information Center

(Map p134; 210-244-2000; www.visitsan antonio.com; 317 Alamo Plaza; 9am-5pm) Staff at this center in San Antonio hand out maps and brochures, answer questions, and distribute tour and VIA bus/ streetcar passes. The website has loads of useful information. Opposite the Alamo.

Visas

○ Visa rules change frequently and travelers should always double-check current requirements at the Department of State (https:// travel.state.gov/visa), where downloadable forms are available.

○ Currently, under the US Visa Waiver Program (VWP), visas are not required for citizens of

40 countries, including the United Kingdom, Australia, New Zealand, EU countries, South Korea and Japan.

○ Citizens of VWP countries must request travel authorization from Electronic System for Travel Authorization (ESTA; https://esta.cbp.dhs.gov) at least 72 hours in advance. Visitors not eligible for the program will require a B-2 tourism visa in advance of their arrival.

○ Visa waiver is good for 90 days, no extensions. You must have an e-Passport with an electronic chip. VWP visitors must register only with the ESTA at least 72 hours before their trip begins. Once approved, ESTA registration is valid for up to two years. If you don't meet any of these requirements, even if your passport is from

one of the listed countries, you'll need a visa to enter the USA. Note that though not a part of the VWP, citizens from Canada do not require a visa for 90-day stays.

○ All foreign visitors who need to obtain a temporary visitor visa (B-2) must do so from a US consulate or embassy abroad. Consult that embassy's website for forms and procedures, which vary by country.

Responsible Travel

Reduce your carbon footprint Opt for trains and buses rather than planes if practical. (Amtrak's Texas Eagle, for instance, travels daily from San Antonio

to Chicago via Austin.) Where possible, take public transportation and explore on foot or bicycle rather than car.

Reduce waste Use a refillable water bottle rather than buying single-use plastic. Carry and use your own bag when making purchases.

Buy local Shop at farmers markets, seek out locally owned restaurants and buy crafts straight from the source. Find trusted local businesses at www.do512.com/p/locally-owned-in-austin.

Avoid overtourism Try to travel outside of peak season (generally March to May and September to October); visit major sights on weekdays rather than weekends.

Behind the Scenes

Send Us Your Feedback

We love to hear from travelers – your comments help make our books better. We read every word, and we guarantee that your feedback goes straight to the authors. Visit **lonelyplanet.com/contact** to submit your updates and suggestions.

Note: We may edit, reproduce and incorporate your comments in Lonely Planet products such as guidebooks, websites and digital products, so let us know if you don't want your comments reproduced or your name acknowledged. For a copy of our privacy policy visit lonelyplanet.com/legal.

Amy's Thanks

Thank you for your Austin recommendations and hospitality: Chris McCray, Doug Kilday, Ken Wiles and family, John Apperson and Amanda Bachman. For fine party throwing and fierce BBQ opinions, thanks to the Austin W&L crew and their families: Jenny Stratton, Anna Salas, Kelly Rogers, Lucy Anderson, Bitsy and David Young, Chris Casey and John Pipkin. Thank you Paul and Crystal Sadler for the San Antonio tips. Finally, thanks to Alex Howard for entrusting me with this awesome assignment.

Acknowledgements

Front cover photograph: Congress Ave at night, Onfokus/Getty Images ©. Sculpture by Craig Hein.

Back cover photograph: Cowboy boots on sale in Austin, Gavin Hellier/Getty Images ©

This Book

This 2nd edition of Lonely Planet's *Pocket Austin* guidebook was researched and written by Amy Balfour, Regis St Louis and Greg Ward. The previous edition was written by Amy Balfour and Stephen Lioy. This guidebook was produced by the following:

Commissioning Editor
Kate Chapman

Product Editor
James Appleton

Cartographer
Hunor Csutoros

Book Designer
Aomi Ito

Assisting Editors
Alex Conroy, Melanie Dankel, Carly Hall, Rosie Nicholson, Gabrielle Stefanos

Cover Researcher
Hannah Blackie

Thanks to Sonia Kapoor, Kate Mathews, Darren O'Connell

Index

See also separate subindexes for:

⊗ **Eating** p158

☺ **Drinking** p159

☺ **Entertainment** p159

🛍 **Shopping** p159

⊗ Eating

Our Writers

Amy Balfour

Amy practiced law in Virginia before moving to Los Angeles to try to break in as a screenwriter. After a stint as a writer's assistant on *Law & Order,* she jumped into freelance writing, focusing on travel, food and the outdoors. Amy has hiked, biked and paddled across the United States, and has crisscrossed Texas in search of the region's best barbecue and outdoor attractions.

Regis St Louis

Regis grew up in a small town in the American Midwest – the kind of place that fuels dreams of travel – and he developed an early fascination with world cultures. He spent his formative years studying various Slavic and Romance languages, which served him well on journeys across much of the globe. Regis has contributed to more than one hundred Lonely Planet titles.

Greg Ward

Since his youthful adventures on the hippy trail to India, and living in northern Spain, Greg has written guides to destinations all over the world. As well as covering the USA from the Southwest to Hawaii, he has ranged on recent assignments from Corsica to the Cotswolds, Dallas to Delphi. Visit his website, www.gregward.info, to see his favourite photos and memories.

Published by Lonely Planet Global Limited
CRN 554153
2nd edition – Dec 2022
ISBN 978 1 78701 614 9
© Lonely Planet 2022   Photographs © as indicated 2022
10 9 8 7 6 5 4 3 2 1
Printed in Malaysia